Finding Passion

A Self-Discovery Approach for Navigating Career Crossroads

JESSICA MANCA

A Managing Mindspaces Book

Copyright© 2013 by Jessica Manca. All rights reserved.

No portion of this book many be reproduced or transmitted in any form or by any means, electronic or mechanical, including photocopying, without permission in writing from the publisher, except for the inclusion of brief quotations in a review.

Limit of Liability/Disclaimer of Warranty: While the publisher and author have used their best efforts in preparing this book, they make no representations or warranties with respect to the accuracy or completeness of the contents of this book and specifically disclaim any implied warranties of merchantability or fitness for a particular purpose. No warranty may be created or extended by sales representatives or written sales materials. The advice and strategies contained herein may not be suitable for your situation. You should consult with a professional where appropriate. Neither the publisher nor author shall be liable for any loss of profit or any other commercial damages, including but not limited to special, incidental, consequential, or other damages.

ISBN - 13: 978-0-9920823-0-7
ISBN - 10: 0-9920823-0-7

Library and Archives Canada

Cover art by Jessica Manca

Published by Managing Mindspaces
Suite #177 1917 West 4th Avenue, Vancouver, British Columbia V6J 1M7
Send inquiries to: publishing@managingmindspaces.com

To all those talented individuals working so hard to fulfill someone else's dream.

CONTENTS

Preface		vii
Acknowledgements		xiii
Introduction		xv
1	**Getting Started**	3
	How to prepare for self-discovery work.	
2	**Daydream**	11
	What did you always want to do?	
3	**Personal Values**	21
	What do you stand for?	
4	**Experience**	31
	What worked, and what didn't?	
5	**Ultimate Future**	43
	What's the legacy you want to leave behind?	
6	**Personal Brand and Narrative**	57
	How do you express your Passion?	
7	**Talent**	69
	What comes naturally to you?	
8	**Authenticity**	77
	How aligned are you to your values?	
9	**Passion**	95
	What's your Passion?	
10	**Action Plan**	103
	How will you bring your Passion forward?	
11	**Bonus—Overcommitment**	113
	How to protect your priorities and action plan	
Conclusion		119
Appendix: Maintenance Program		123
About the Author		128

PREFACE

Just because I'm good at my job, doesn't mean my job is good for me.
- Jessica Manca

I felt like an impostor. I was lost, and I had lost touch with myself. Deep down I knew it was partly my own doing. How did I get here, and how could I get free? The circumstances at work and at home forced a conversation that I had long been avoiding. I didn't know how to ask myself what I really wanted for my life and career. I just knew this wasn't it.

My experience losing my way was so transformative that I had to write a book about what I went through. In the process of writing this book, I've had colleagues whisper, "Jessica, I had no idea this happened. I thought I was the only one." One colleague said life had passed her by. Another said he had reached his limit and thought work would kill him.

I wrote this book to help others learn what they really want to accomplish in their careers. I remember how much energy I spent thinking about what to do before taking action. I know how dire it feels to want answers now. I know how constant stress can cloud your judgment and keep you feeling stuck.

I believe that you can live your ultimate future, and that the career crossroads you face is just a temporary hurdle.

Whatever brought you to this crossroads, trust me when I say you're not alone. In this book, I'll share everything I know to be true about resolving inner conflict and making lasting personal change. I'll reveal my innermost thoughts and expose information that I've never shared before. Through my courage to write these words, I hope that I can inspire you to follow my example and set yourself free.

I want to share how I found my Passion. It's because of this story, I'm able to reach you now.

The Surprising Event That Got Me Here

I was at the top of my game. My consulting career was in hyper-drive. My experience had grown tenfold in the last several years as I worked on technology implementations with increased accountability. I had such a sense of belonging with other like-minded, high performers who delivered quality and value. Work was my identity.

I was rewarded well for my effort. Performance review feedback each year was outstanding and often tops within my level of the firm. There were substantial bonuses for outperforming my peers. I drank the corporate Kool-Aid and morphed into the ideal employee. Without a mid-career female role model similar to me, I developed an unrealistic picture of what I should be within the company.

In my experience working in IT, there aren't many examples of those who can sustain the pace of consulting work during the early years of starting a family. I did have two male mentors whose children were older and had a healthy work/life balance. The equivalent female mentor didn't exist in my office. Women typically move to part-time, step away for a few years, or dread that starting a family will make their career come to an screeching halt. I wanted to figure it out. Just as when taking on a complex project, I wanted to step up and show everyone that I could have both career and family.

When the time came to come back to work from twelve months of maternity leave in Canada, I didn't expect life to change much. I expected to get my next promotion to senior management rather quickly. Major miscalculation on my part. I forced an outcome without fully understanding the role my identity would play.

The most difficult experience of my career

Five months after returning to work, I was pleased things were running smoothly. My schedule calibrated into a new daily routine. My workweek was around forty hours per week, which was a nice pace. Still I felt guilty for the time lost while away. Others had gotten promoted in the meantime, and I felt behind.

My opportunity to catch up came when I was offered a role on a long-term project with a respected and relentless leadership team. Three partners asked me to do the firm a favor and fill the position. The role tested my ability to manage a very sizable contract. I remember thinking, this is the kind of opportunity that would test anyone to the limits. My competitive side gladly accepted the role.

Not only had I set the expectations that I liked challenging work, I arrogantly asked my leaders to push me to grow even further. I wanted to fully seize the opportunity in front of me. The challenge, the expectations, and the upcoming promotion created a perfect storm burnout.

Within less than two weeks of being assigned to the project, I found my work was anything but smooth. I thought I thrived under high pressure. I began feeling very overwhelmed. I couldn't escape that feeling each day.

That early stage of burnout looked like this: I felt uneasy every day, unsure of what was important or a priority. I second-guessed myself. I was what I used to call beyond stressed. I was "crispy-fried." My energy levels and focus were completely absent, and I couldn't manage my time anymore. I developed a shorter fuse, to put it nicely, and the smallest of things would set me off.

There was another change happening. I lost my ability to speak up. Careful not to draw attention to my feelings of inadequacy, I rarely shared my opinion. That was a big shift. I used to be an employee you could count on for speaking the truth and telling it like it is. My confidence was slipping.

It was a large workload and a project that required more like a fourteen-hour day, with occasional weekend work as well. Within such a short time, I felt as if I were weeks behind schedule. It was a constant feeling of catch-up to establish consistent team performance, quality controls and reporting to the degree that was expected. I was stuck in the fear that I needed to ask for help, but couldn't. Reaching out for help would have made me look as if I couldn't handle it.

The time I spent at work was taking a toll on my family. I leaned on my husband so much. I barely had energy left to spend quality time with either him or my son. There was no time, really, for my personal life other than eating and sleeping in order to gear up for the next day at work.

This feeling went on for nearly nine months. My performance in the role kept unraveling me. I was dropping the ball all over the place. I butted heads with one peer in particular so often, that it felt as if I was at war.

All eyes were on me—the leadership, the team, and the younger women with whom I worked with closely were all watching me. Female colleagues would tell me that if anyone could make motherhood and a consulting career work while making the next level, I was the one to figure it out. I didn't have the courage to admit that this could end my career in consulting altogether.

Before I knew it, I stopped functioning and completely shut down.

Doing as instructed like a robot

I held my head up high, thinking I'd just try harder. Unsure if it it was just work/life balance, I went on autopilot. I did whatever was asked of me. Like a robot, I suppressed all feelings and intuition to get the work done. This horrible shell started to build around me, protecting me and hiding the fact that I was miserable. I was putting on the biggest show of my life.

I tried other things too. I tried saying no to new assignments, but then gave in to doing what I was told. I tried to delegate and leverage the skills of my team yet micromanaged capable team members. I was conflicted, and my actions showed it. I can see now how hard I used to be on myself. In my journal, my fear of being exposed showed through. "*No mistakes,*" I wrote.

The more I tried to resist the pressure, the more burned out I felt. In the past, it wasn't uncommon for me to experience burnout as a consultant, but the quick wins and short-term nature of the work would get me over that feeling quickly. I'd forget the pain and start the cycle again.

In another entry I vented, "*Extreme rage. 'K' volunteered me for something new...but feel really good overall. Getting on track, meeting deadlines. I like my job again.*" As with a yo-yo diet, I was in a love-hate relationship with my job. "*Long day. Trying to step up. I think I've been too lax on myself, and it's not working either,*" I wrote.

Zombie-like numbness

I worked with one of my male mentors to discuss ways for finding balance, assuming this was just a passing phase. I recall saying that I wanted to harness my energy, and I felt scattered like I was pulled in too many different directions. He wanted to know my hobbies outside of work. I gave him a wide-eyed, blank stare.

"*I'm not supposed to be doing this,*" I thought. I was tired of the charade. By month seven, I had drastically cut my hair short, and my stylist asked about the sudden change. He said that usually when people cut their hair, something major's happening in their life. It was a great question, but I stubbornly dismissed the comment. "*How dare he assume he knows what I'm going through.*"

I felt broken, as my mental exhaustion turned into physical exhaustion. I was sluggish, gaining weight, and numbing myself with drinking daily. I no longer recognized the person I saw in the mirror. Worse, I would dream about work. The key players in the project would show up in my sleep when I was trying to rest from it all. I'd wake up exhausted with no desire to go into the office. Work was toxic to me, and I didn't understand how a job that had worked so well for me in the past could give me such an intense anxiety attack.

I've referred to my journal several times in recounting my story because even to this day, my mind protects me from these highly emotional experiences. Right before the annual performance review, I wrote, "*I didn't act my best today. I just feel defeated. Nothing can save this other than to get away.*"

My feedback was much different that year. It was the first time that I didn't get high marks. I was warned I had almost received the mark "IPR" for Improved Performance Required. Human Resources spoke with me, and there was some talk of an action plan to get me back on track, although it was never determined what exactly that plan needed to be. Without a straight answer on what I could have done to improve, the feedback reinforced my belief that I was forever broken.

Mortified and devastated, I confided in my loving husband, who expressed how much this job was affecting the three of us. I was giving so much to work and leaving nothing for my family. I was a zombie of my former self, and I grew resentful of the burden of being a mother trying to keep up a career. I was so stressed out that I was starting to not care anymore, and it was getting scary.

I remember my husband saying, "Take ten seconds and tell me what you want to do." I told him I wanted to move back west to where we'd met. I also knew in my heart I wanted to leave the company. This conversation cemented my commitment to freeing myself.

My turning point

We began planning our move west, and I began planning my departure from the firm. Once I admitted there was a big problem, I realized that I needed outside help to make it through the ordeal of telling my partners and deciding next steps.

I first hired a therapist who helped me cope with the situation I was still working in. She helped me to look back at what she called "triggers" while at work. We talked extensively about my emotions, replayed key events, and unpacked the parts of me that emerged while defending myself at work. Our goal was to understand the anxiety in a way that I could better self-manage in the future should the pattern come up again.

With each new piece of understanding and self awareness, I began to smile more. I began to feel more myself in my own skin. Little sparks of the happy person I used to be would come out. There was much healing to do, the therapist and I worked together for several months on rebuilding my trust in myself to manage my actions. "*I am my own light,*" became my new motto meaning that I'm always there for myself no matter what.

As we completed our work together, I had learned how to cope and thought I needed help in figuring out what was next for my career. Working with someone who could provide an outside perspective moved me forward faster than I could move alone. Asking for help felt so good because I knew I was doing something about my situation and not playing a victim. Why didn't I ask for help before?

Proud that I was able to leave on good terms and move to a less intense project during my final weeks, I researched a professional certified coach in the Vancouver area. I wanted to find the answers about what people in this situation do with their careers. What were my options? What would make me happy?

Could I ever trust myself?

Trusting myself was the biggest shift I made in my thinking. I knew upfront that the project role was demanding and maybe more than I could handle. My actions and intentions helped create that toxic environment, and I made so many choices that made the situation awful. After the first coaching session, I felt capable of bouncing back to achieve even greater things in my life. I would be my own role model moving forward.

Had I not gone through these experiences so intensely, I would still be in my corporate position, trying to make it fit my new lifestyle and wondering why I was working my life away.

The unlimited rewards of finding my Passion

During the process of figuring out what I wanted with the help of a coach, I found so much more. I found my Passion. I reunited with my true self again. I rediscovered the things that excited me. I felt happier, lighter. It was as if I had learned a little secret for getting unstuck, and just the thought of it made me smile. My husband said that I was reminding him of the person he met a decade ago.

A few other things changed as well. I found my voice again. My decision-making ability and confidence improved. My judgment was much less clouded by what others thought or by trying to say the "right" answer. I harnessed my energy toward what's important for me, not what was urgent for others. I started to live in alignment with my values on a daily basis. I started to be more present and alive when spending time with my family.

So when friends were surprised that we sold our dream house and moved cross-country without jobs, this leap of faith felt so right to me. I knew I'd land on my feet after I took that leap.

ACKNOWLEDGMENTS

Thank you to every colleague, client, and friend who contributed to this body of work.

Thank you to the growing profession of coaching, which gave me the gift to find the best solution from within. Thank you for the gift of finding myself again, so much so that I became a coach to do the same for others.

Special thanks to the courageous individuals who shared their stories, achieved many acts of courage, and kept the commitment to themselves to find their answers.

Unlimited gratitude to my mom, dad, sister, and Lovus for your support in this and many chapters to come.

INTRODUCTION

Inner freedom is not guided by our efforts; it comes from seeing what is true.
- The Buddha

Whatever brought you to this moment, I want to assure you that everything you need to change you already have. Finding Passion helps you explore what you really want to do with your career by asking challenging questions. The book gets right into the work. There's no fluff because I know you don't want to waste any more energy waiting in limbo.

Overview

This workbook is designed for individuals at the crossroads of contemplating a career change, experiencing a transition or feeling the urge for something greater. By finding your Passion, you'll feel confident you have the information you need to make informed decisions within your career. During this process, you'll get back to the roots of who you are and what you want.

Designed for career scenarios

Specifically, the book caters to the following needs:

- Reaching a life milestone such as finding a partner, starting a family, being mid-career or preretirement;

- Feeling unfulfilled in a well-paying job and daydreaming about other opportunities;

- Feeling unmotivated and bored with unchallenging work that leaves you craving something new;

- Fearing how to handle success or how to deal with failure reaching for your big dreams, and

- Knowing what you want and feeling ready to bring your vision, movement, or business to life.

By the end of the book, you'll have discovered your Passion, which means you will know what you want, live in alignment to your future vision, and leap over the career crossroads you face.

Philosophy

In creating the exercises within the workbook, I was profoundly influenced by an improved understanding of the stages for personal change. This model helps to shape the structure of the book, along with professional coaching and other principles described.

Stages of Personal Change

A person passes through a series of stages for behavioral change, each increasing the person's readiness for the next stage. According to John Prochaska's Transtheoretical Model of Change, there are six stages: Precontemplation, Contemplation, Preparation, Action, Maintenance, and Integration.

The workbook takes you through Preparation, Action, and Maintenance. In the time before you bought the book, you passed the Precontemplation and Contemplation stages, where ideas of making a change have been percolating for some time. By now, you have determined to make a change.

According to Prochaska's research across the last thirty-five years, if an individual is pushed into action too quickly, that person will resist. The change process supports allowing individuals to work up to action and to advance at their own pace. Similarly, the book ramps up to action and encourages you to do as much or as little as you need. You're the judge of when you're ready to begin any or all of this work and can slow when you need to or speed up when you get excited at what you discover.

Professional Coaching

Professional coaching is a forward-focused, goal-driven approach to managing personal change. Coaching finds the solution within, using powerful questions to facilitate learning. A coach provides you an objective observer when the truth is hidden, and the consequence of remaining "stuck" is no longer an option.

Working with a professional coach helps individuals reach goals and reframe their perspective. Coaching begins with an interview, in-person or via phone, to discuss challenges, opportunities, priorities for the individual, and desired outcomes for coaching. Subsequent coaching sessions work within the boundaries of the agreement. The length of the coaching relationship varies depending on the needs and preferences of the individual; however, most coaching programs range from three to six months.

Listed below are the most common benefits described by individuals who hire a coach.

- Improved decision-making skills working with a coach as a thinking partner

- Uncover blind spots and disrupt patterns of behavior, building confidence

- Be held accountable for actions for increased attainment of desired goals

- Improved work life balance, communication, performance, or time management

While there are many type of coaches, such as business, executive, career, or life coaches, *Finding Passion* primarily supports a process for sensible coaching across the intersection of life and career areas. Breakthrough or "aha" moments are expected to help shift your perspective allowing you to move forward at your own pace.

Trusted, certified coaches

The International Coach Federation (ICF) is the recognized global leader in accepted industry standards and advancement of the coaching profession. While there may be many individuals using the term "coach" to describe their services, the coach context we'll be referring to in this book is one who is a certified coach by the ICF. "A coach who has been credentialed by the ICF has completed stringent education and experience requirements and has demonstrated a strong commitment to excellence in coaching," as defined by the Federation.

There are three credentials that inform consumers that a coach is proficient and abides by the competencies and ethics set forth by the ICF. Recognized and trusted designations include Associate Certified Coach (ACC), Professional Certified Coach (PCC), and Master Certified Coach (MCC).

While there are many coaches holding independent and institution-specific degrees, the ICF explains that an ICF credentialed coach comes with a "highly recognizable, global coaching qualification. Coaches credentialed by ICF have received coach-specific training, have achieved a designated number of experience hours, and been coached by a Mentor Coach."

Other Key Principles Used

Additional principles behind the design of this book work together to create a learning environment for your self-discovery. Below is a high-level overview of the key principles.

Using a coach approach

The language chosen neutralizes any perceived judgment or directive. The workbook provides open-ended questions to enable you to explore possibilities without being prescribed a solution. The examples used are from my personal transformation to support the place of vulnerability you need to reach to find your answers and face your truth. These examples may provide you with ideas, but should not be interpreted as the best way to move forward.

Leveraging your learning styles

A learning style reflects a person's natural pattern of acquiring and processing information in learning situations. Whether you think in pictures, learn through listening, or prefer to learn by experience or writing, you will find exercises in the workbook that tap into your learning style. By asking you to draw, daydream, and fill in the blank, the exercises will prompt you to use your creativity while meeting the learning objectives of each chapter.

Experimenting and adapting to what works

Feel free to modify suggested practices so you can use the learning style that works best for you.

A Roadmap for Your Journey

The book follows a sequence of steps in the chapters that follow to build your readiness for finding your Passion. A roadmap is shown at the start of each chapter to help you track how far you've come within the stages of personal change.

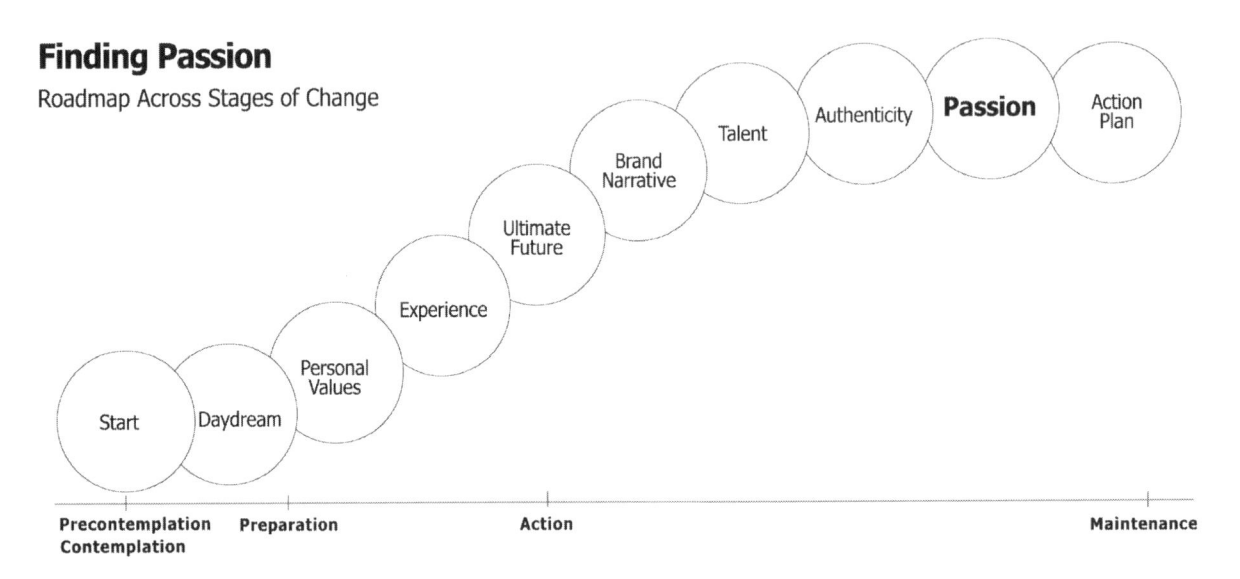

Figure 1. *Finding Passion* Roadmap across the stages of change.

Chapter Summary

In *Finding Passion*, you'll shorten the learning curve to the crossroads you face and make confident decisions as to your next steps. Here's how the chapters break down:

- **Chapter 1** – Preparation for self-discovery work;

- **Chapters 2–4** – Expressing what you want, what's important you, what you've learned;

- **Chapter 5** – Articulating your long-term vision;

- **Chapter 6** – Taking action and sharing your Passion with others;

- **Chapter 7** – Identifying your natural talent;

- **Chapter 8** – Checking authenticity for alignment;

- **Chapter 9** – Finding Passion;
- **Chapter 10** – Building a sensible plan; and
- **Chapter 11** – A bonus chapter for managing distractions.

Your Commitment

I feel that finding your Passion is the answer to so many of the questions you have about your future. The book includes essential self-discovery questions to help you conduct an interview with yourself in search of your answer. The exercises require you to self-reflect and increase self-awareness by looking inward and forward.

Knowing oneself is an ongoing project and not a one-time effort. It's very easy to return back to default reactions and behavior when faced with adversity while reaching for a Passion.

The stories shared within the book come from my experience during this process. I continue to use these exercises both in my ongoing personal development and with my clients, who desire more meaning to their careers, increased work/life balance, and living with integrity to their values. Most often they discover their inner strengths, get to know themselves again, and find out how they can be intentional in their lives.

I strongly believe in being coached to hold me accountable to my vision and to help me see when old thinking collides with my goals. I continue to work with a coach twice a month and always feel lighter and more compassionate towards myself as I continue on my journey.

You'll need to bring your energy, your drive, your commitment, and your openness in order to kick start the change you seek. Are you ready?

Finding Passion

Chapter 1

GETTING STARTED

We meet ourselves time and again in a thousand disguises on the path of life.
- Carl Jung

In this chapter, you'll learn:

- What self-discovery is

- How to practice self-discovery and reflective thinking

- What to expect across the book and with written exercises

- How to plan for ongoing Maintenance of the work

You're shifting from Contemplation to Preparation.

Finding Passion
Roadmap Across Stages of Change

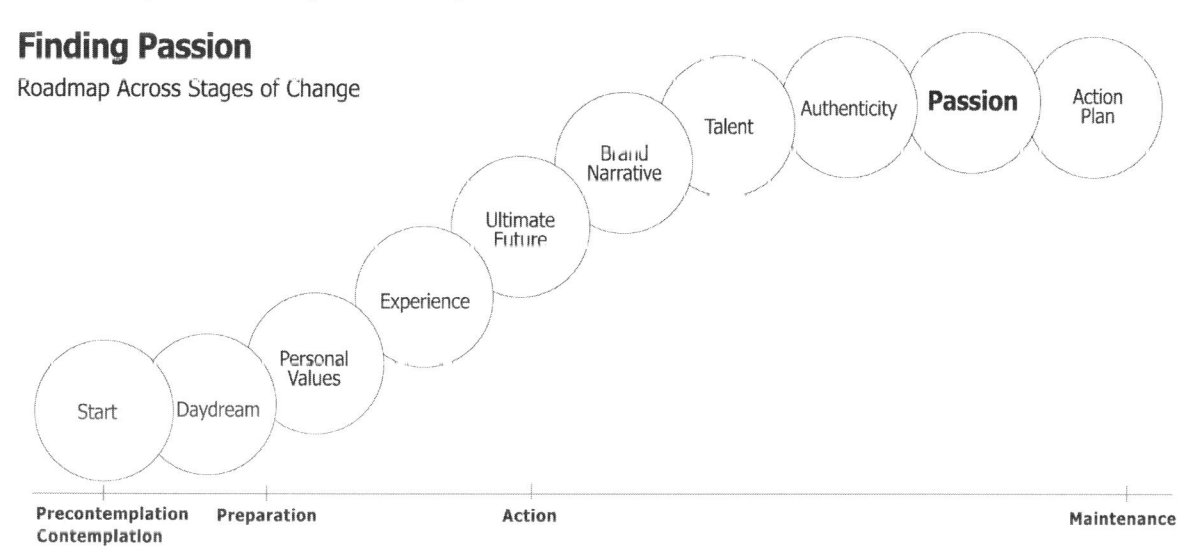

Start → Daydream → Personal Values → Experience → Ultimate Future → Brand Narrative → Talent → Authenticity → **Passion** → Action Plan

Precontemplation/Contemplation — Preparation — Action — Maintenance

Figure 2. *Finding Passion* Roadmap, entering the Preparation stage for change.

Getting Started

At a point in life, many of us question our path. We achieve, reach, and soar only to find ourselves later stuck at another crossroads. This is our journey, which, it seems, we repeat across our lifetime. This journey is learning.

The first step in learning is preparation, which is also the stage of personal change you're entering. This chapter ensures you understand the nature of the work ahead, what to expect, and some practices which you can start right away.

What's Self-Discovery?

Self-discovery awaits you in the pages of *Finding Passion*. Unlike approaches recommended in other self-help resources, self-discovery allows you to better understand yourself through increasing your awareness. There's no prescribed solution here. There's no right answers or magic potion to finding your Passion. As you can imagine, finding Passion is an incredibly delicate and personal quest.

Rather than passively receiving advice, you'll learn insights into what's essential for you. Ideas may return to the forefront of your thinking. Emotions may stir and even surprise you. This is expected. You'll decide what's valuable and what to carry forward with you.

Each of us must be courageous and vulnerable to take on self-discovery work. The ability to ask ourselves tough questions allows us to see our strengths, our weaknesses, our drivers, and our values. Self-awareness also helps us see what impact we have on each other and our larger part in the world.

Once we're ready for self-discovery, we find helpful friends who've been there before. When we're ready to listen to what our friends share, we see that we're not alone.

Practices for Self-Discovery

In preparing, you'll need to choose a method of capturing your notes. You'll need to be a student again, collecting insights, observations, and feelings as they appear. Your note taking will be an extension of the self-reflection done with the book. Make any of these strategies a daily or weekly practice while working with *Finding Passion*. Here are six suggestions to help you.

Journaling

Find paper and pen. Start writing. There are no fixed rules to journaling. Write what you want, when you want. Let off steam, or spill your deepest secrets. It only has to make sense to you.

Engage a friend

If you like to talk it out, engage a friend to share what you're experiencing. Your friend can be your sounding board and sparring partner on several of the exercises, as noted in the instructions prior to each exercise.

Voice or video recording

Use the voice or video recorder on your phone or computer to record your thoughts and expressions.

Drawings

If you like to create, find a sketchbook, paint, or clay. Who says your answers need to be written?

Photography

Capture a self-portrait every day. Capture a comment about your Passion. Would there be a noticeable change in you once you had the answers you were seeking?

Social media sharing

Post your comments to Facebook or Twitter. Reveal a different part of yourself to your friends and recognize your achievements. Use #FindingPassionBook to connect with fellow readers going through their self-discovery.

Preparing for Reflective Thinking

To get the most from the book, prepare each time you sit down to start a chapter. Work at a pace and style that feels comfortable. Come back to these steps to get into this mindset each time you pick up the book.

- **Clear your mind of distractions.** Sit in a creative place or quiet setting that is different than what you would normally choose. Changing your vantage point helps change your perspective.

- **Mix it up.** Grab a different-colored pen, pencil, or marker—one that you rarely use. Working with a new writing utensil disrupts your patterns and facilitates your ability to think differently. Using a marker helps you write simply using fewer words.

- **Be honest with yourself.**

- **Trust your instincts.** Don't over-think the exercises. Write the first answers that come to you.

- **Let loose.** Remember your answers will not be graded, judged, nor compared to others'. Resist the urge to "make it pretty" or sound impressive. Instead, get real.

Chapter Design and Written Work

Each chapter begins with an inspirational quote and learning objective to orient you. With minimal preamble, the summary goes right into preparing you for the exercises with instructions and tips. There's at least one exercise per chapter for you to focus on. Following the exercise, there are required questions to deepen your understanding. Finally, each chapter ends with space for taking additional notes, if you choose.

You may write your answers directly in the book, at the end of the chapters within designated Notes pages, or you may use your preferred tool for practicing self-discovery such as journal, voice recorder, or a friend with a good memory. Rather than remind you of the six methods described at the start of each exercise, the book will refer to your "notes" as the method you've chosen.

Mindspaces Door icon

There are open-ended questions throughout the book to explore possibilities and new thinking. These questions are signified by the Mindspaces Door icon.

The Mindspaces Door icon represents your connection to the unlimited possibilities in your mind. Mindspaces is a synonym for brain power or the place where you hold all your mindsets. These questions help you assess, draw out, and reframe your thinking. Try practicing with the sample question below and with Exercise 1 on the next page.

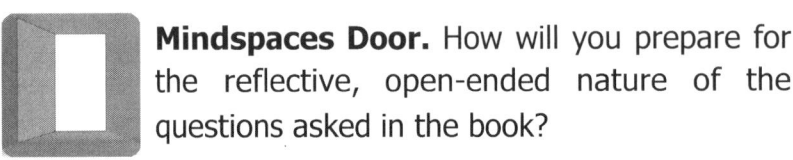

Mindspaces Door. How will you prepare for the reflective, open-ended nature of the questions asked in the book?

Figure 3. Sample Mindspaces coaching question.

Maintaining Your Passion

Finding Passion is designed to be a continuous self-discovery tool for navigating career crossroads. The work itself is iterative and can be repeated to increase clarity whenever you need it.

Revisit these exercises on a regular basis. Reviewing your answers helps you refine your meaning of Passion and what's important to you. More on maintenance later in the Appendix.

Picture of Possibilites | Exercise 1

As you proceed through the book, you're going to need not only the vision for your Passion, but also a picture of calming, positive energy. This image is the picture of possibilities. It may be palm trees at the beach, wildflowers in a rolling meadow, or a majestic mountain top. Whatever peaceful place that comes to mind for you, this image will be a point of reference any time you want some relaxation to get you in the mindset of reflective thinking.

Preparation

- Review the five tips in Preparing for Reflective Thinking in the previous section.

Instructions

(1) Think of the word "possibilities," and close your eyes for ten seconds.

(2) Allow your mind to paint a picture. What appears?

(3) Describe and draw your picture(s) on the next page.

Picture of Possibilites | Exercise 1

When I think of possibilities, I see _____.

Required Self-Discovery

Meeting Expectations. When you reach the end of the workbook, what do you want to have achieved?

Notes

Chapter 2

DAYDREAMING

Our life is shaped by the mind; we become what we think.
- Buddha

In this chapter, you'll learn:

- How dreams hold clues to your Passion
- Which common barriers get in the way of daydreaming

You are in the Preparation stage and are ready to start.

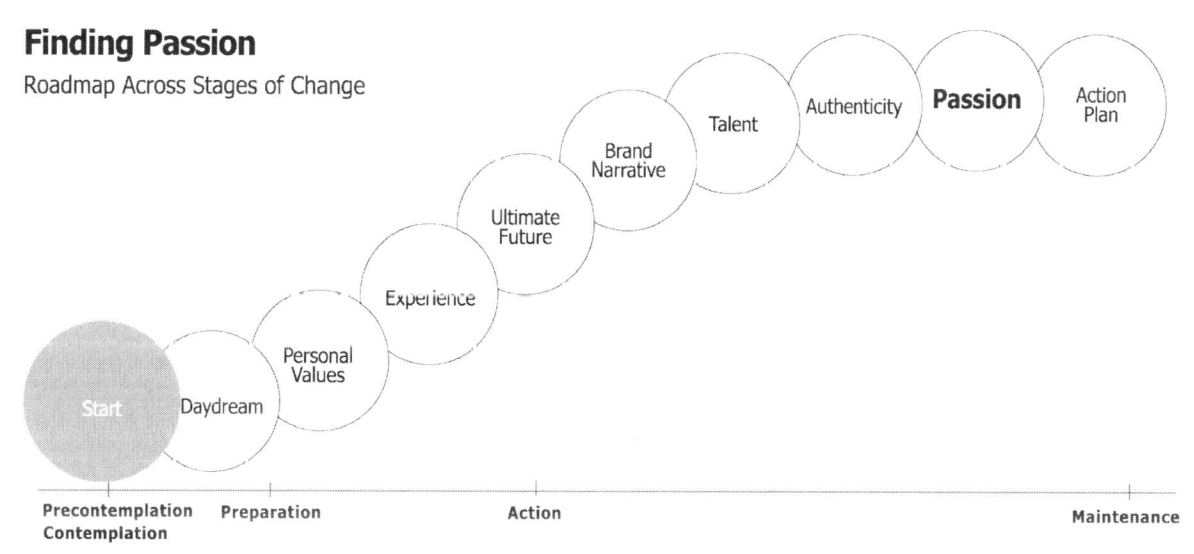

Figure 4. *Finding Passion* Roadmap, ready to start your Preparation.

Daydreaming

Now that you're set up, you're going to tap into all data available, including your dreams. Your dreams, both day and night, may hold clues for finding your Passion.

Passion is fire, energy, desire, and excitement! It's flair, zest, and spice! We have Passion when it doesn't matter how long something takes. We have Passion when we show up in the pouring rain because we want to be there. We have Passion when even the thought of something makes us light up and gain energy. Take a hard listen to the thoughts and images coming to mind right now.

That energy comes from within, which is why knowing what questions to ask ourselves makes for a difficult task. That's where the next exercise can help prompt you to recall visions, images, and dreams you've once had about your Passion.

What to watch out for

It's worth mentioning that there are a few barriers that may come into play at this step, such as fears, limited thinking, and seeking permission. To prevent these barriers from blocking your ability to reflect, we're going to call them out so you can recognize them should they appear. Record in your Notes any areas you'll be watching for.

- **Fear.** You may have a fear of the unknown, the future, success, or failure. A fear can reinforce the story you tell yourself that you can't have Passion. Think about whether you're ready and willing to conquer this fear as part of the work.

- **Limited thinking.** Don't allow the "How" to get in the way of stating the "What." Are you overwhelmed with how your Passion will manifest? Let go of thinking that says this work is ambitious or too far-fetched to achieve. In this chapter, anything is possible.

- **Permission.** While permission doesn't seem like an obvious barrier to overcome, you may recognize that the person you want permission from is yourself. In our busy careers, we get accustomed to getting permission from our senior leaders. In this case, the senior leader is you.

> ### Passion's Patience
>
> The first time I sat down to evaluate what my next career would look like, I ran into each of the three types of barriers listed above. I had a fear of the unknown and of success. I had a fear of how I would find my next opportunity in a new city. I even had a strange feeling that I needed to check with someone to make sure my decision was all right.
>
> Over my career, I was trained to take projects and implement them. I wasn't typically designing them. As I was accustomed to, I wanted to implement an already designed "find a new career and get a job plan," but no such plan existed.
>
> I foolishly began searching for a position without knowing what I wanted for a career. Even more, I looked for identical jobs to the one I had just left. "Just in case," I would say.
>
> Each time I evaluated options, the question kept coming back to "What do I really want?" It's

> much easier to make a plan to change careers by seeing what's out there than it is to answer this one question. My Passion waited patiently as I finally answered it.
>
> It was at this point, I decided to work with a coach to broaden my thinking.

Remembering Dreams | Exercise 2

This exercise conjures up some big ideas you've had that may have merit when it comes to finding your Passion. If you ever wanted to be a famous race car driver, a rock star or a dancer, hang onto those ideas, no matter how farfetched they may seem.

Preparation

- Clear your mind from all lingering doubts. You're beginning from a new starting point that is kind, gentle, and open to all possibilities.

- Try to put your fears aside for the next few pages.

- Grant yourself permission to daydream. Let go of the "how," and just focus on the "what."

- Try to answer each question. If at any point you find yourself saying, "I don't know," take a pause. Come back to this question when ready. Now is the time to articulate what you do know.

- Try using a marker or crayon for the next exercise. Get creative.

Instructions

(1) Start this exercise from the Picture of Possibilities you mentioned on page 8. With your image in mind, begin Exercise 2.

(2) Mark the date you complete this exercise. You'll come back to this in Chapter 10, "Action Plan."

(3) Complete Exercise 2, and remember to use your notes for additional thoughts.

Note: Consider recording your dreams at night as you remember them. Keep your notes near your bed, and write down your dreams in a log. Who was in them, what happened, and how you felt are great pieces to capture.

Remembering Dreams | Exercise 2

Today's date:

(a) Who are the people you admire who are living their Passion?

(b) The glimpses you see of your dream job are:

(c) What comes to mind when you think about your Passion?

Remembering Dreams | Exercise 2

(d) What do you believe you were meant to do?

(e) What would you spend thousands of hours doing in order to gain mastery?

(f) What's the legacy you'd like to leave in the world?

Reviewing What Worked

With Exercise 2 Remembering Dreams, you were given a couple of techniques to help you think about your Passion in a new way. To let the creativity out, your energy and the environment around you are important. You may have discovered:

- **Practice patience.** Daydreaming cannot be rushed.

- **Dedicated time.** Daydreaming cannot be frequently interrupted and is best done in a quiet place.

- **Mix it up.** Using a different-colored marker, pen, or crayon started to influence you to think differently.

- **Get grounded.** Grounding yourself with positive images helped shift your energy from a mindset of frustration to a mindset of possibilities.

Daydreaming serves as a great technique to think about your Passion. Whenever you come across a technique or tool that works for you, feel free to use it again not only in this workbook, but also in your daily practice.

Required Self-Discovery

Observation. What themes did you notice coming from your daydream?

Required Self-Discovery

(a) What makes the questions in Exercise 2 hard to answer, if applicable?

(b) Whose voice gets in the way of finding your Passion (parent, partner, boss, self, other)?

(c) What encouragement would the people you named in Exercise 2 a give to support you?

Notes

Chapter 3

PERSONAL VALUES

When you believe in a thing, believe in it all the way, implicitly and unquestionable.
- Walt Disney

In this chapter, you'll learn:

- How personal values support lasting change
- The benefits of living in alignment with personal values
- How to define your personal values

You are in the Preparation stage and ready to take small steps.

Finding Passion
Roadmap Across Stages of Change

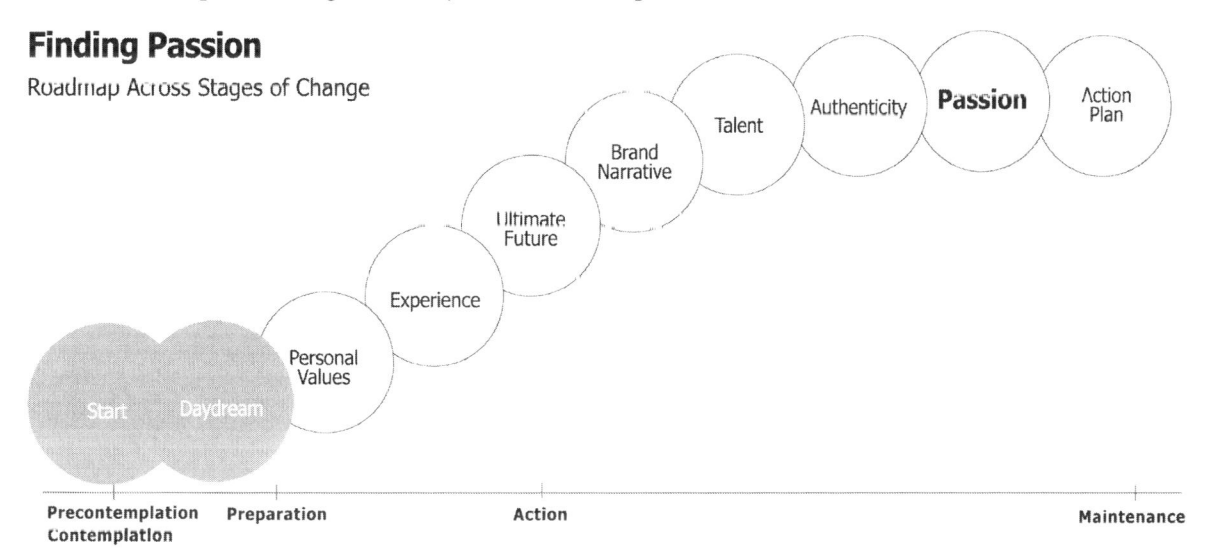

Figure 5. *Finding Passion* Roadmap, continuing within the Preparation stage of change.

Personal Values

Think of personal values as an inner compass that guide a person from the inside out. Values fill a person's essence, and without question, indicate where the heart lies when defining Passion. These values are a combination of beliefs, behaviors, principles, and personality. Values may be the deal-breaking reason for decisions made in life. These values are a constant, present in a person's life as a reliable source of what is held most true.

Understanding personal values is critical to make lasting change. As you're driven deep down by these values, then there's a connection to your outward behavior and actions. If you're not clear on what you value, then how can you decide what you really want?

Living in alignment

Ideally, we strive to live in alignment with our values, making the conditions ripe for our happiness and fulfillment. When you don't live in alignment, there's a self-created wall that lies between what you do and what you value. This wall is conflict and causes feelings of anxiety, discomfort, or stress. The wall suppresses happiness and fulfillment, as it represents a less than optimal outcome for the situation being faced.

This chapter focuses on naming your personal values. If you have done this type of exercise in the past or can name your values now, please continue with the exercise and related questions. You may discover something new, and rekindle the power of the words for you.

Values Reflect What I Stand For

I had always wanted to define my personal values. So when my coach asked me what I valued, I had a general idea yet couldn't name my personal values.

I had been curious to see what impact they could have on me at a time when I was looking for answers. We worked with general concepts, and it wasn't until my coach training that I defined my personal values.

Figure 6. My personal values are truth, interconnectedness and essence.

I started by looking at a list of personal values, and a few jumped out at me. The three values selected were nonnegotiable for living my life. I'm continuing to know myself (Truth), and to share and inspire others (Interconnectedness) before returning to a mindset of simplicity for my life (Essence).

My values connect a compelling need to confront issues head-on by speaking Truths. Interconnectedness means I'm learning, sharing, and appreciating what I have in common with others. I'm attracted to organization and systems for things that are complex. Without these values, I wouldn't be the person that I aspire to be, and already am.

When I had been stressed, I had lost touch with these values. I had carried on in a state of denial, had remained isolated, and had continued to work in complexity.

If I'm living in alignment with my values, I believe:

- **Truth**. Truth is facing what "is," being vulnerable, and exposing fears. The value of Truth is being able to challenge my understanding. Truth develops through self-awareness within positive and negative circumstances.

- **Interconnectedness**. I'm on the same human journey as others who've been there before, and I can only know this by being authentic. By communicating with others, I can see I'm not alone.

- **Essence**. Essence mediates complexity in my life and my thinking, simplifying problems to their origin and returning to refine the Truth as I know it.

Your Inner Compass | Exercise 3

This exercise is simple and empowering. The simplicity is coming up with your personal values. What's empowering is what you do with these values once defined.

Preparation

- Take a scan of the Personal Values List, Table 1, on the next page. Circle the values that resonate with you or grab some post-it notes and write each of your favorite values on a different note for sorting later.

- Take your time. You may find there are many that you're attracted to, so you'll need to evaluate your selection until you've reached the essential five or less. You're looking for specific, exact-meaning words that capture the values you live by.

- Trust your instinct to select the words that come to mind quickly.

- Catch yourself choosing what's politically correct. Give yourself permission to express your values, not the values of others. This workbook is for you. You'll get the most out of the process by putting yourself first.

Instructions

(1) Choose from any of the values listed or create your own for Exercise 3. Write your values inside the compass image or place your post-it notes on the compass image. If you choose, you may put your number one value near the north end of the compass.

(2) After you have an initial list, you might expand or collapse words into alternate categories. If you listed both "Learning" and "Communication," you may revise your value to the broader category of "Wisdom."

Your Inner Compass | Exercise 3 | Personal Values List

Table 1. Personal Values List

\	PERSONAL VALUES	\	\
Happiness	Tradition	Truth	Humor
Wisdom	Decisiveness	Courage	Grace
Respect	Learning	Beauty	Wonder
Trust	Love	Creativity	Connectedness
Integrity	Faith	Health	Optimism
Generosity	Friendliness	Helpfulness	Balance
Adventure	Gratitude	Inspiration	Recognition
Loyalty	Harmony	Success	Calm
Essence	Wealth	Satisfaction	Freedom
Quality	Sharing	Giving	Security
Safety	Justice	Adaptability	Compassion
Power	Simplicity	Mindfulness	Listening
Nurturing	Humanitarianism	Conquest	Patience
Moderation	Spirituality	Practicality	Service
Understanding	Devotion	Focus	Commitment
Organization	Imagination	Determination	Confidence
Flexibility	Purity	Openness	Kindness
Honor	Fun	Leadership	Tolerance
Cooperation	Perseverance	Honestly	Acceptance

PERSONAL VALUES

Your Inner Compass | Exercise 3

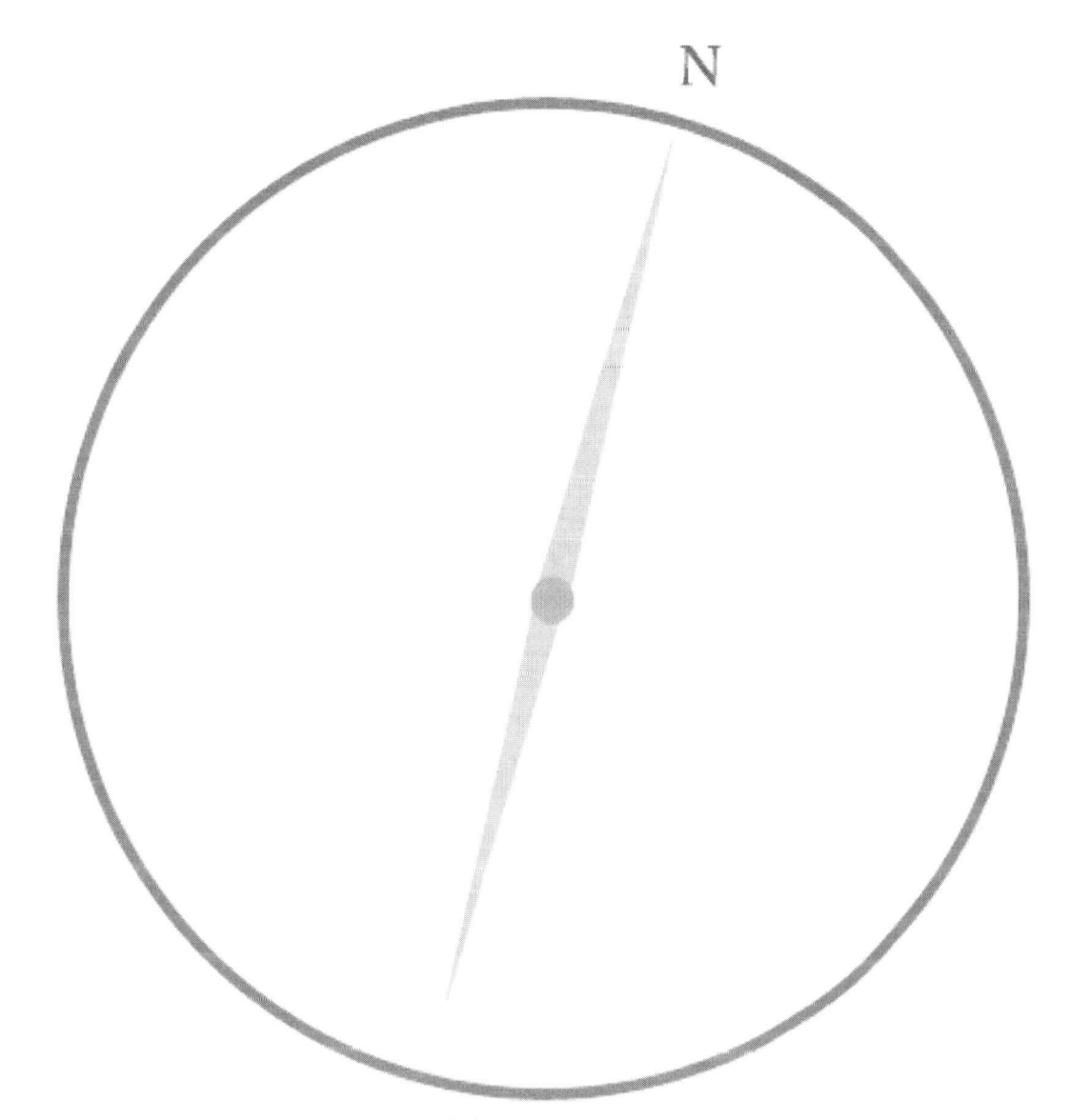

Figure 7. Your personal values serve as an inner compass to guide you.

Feel free to update your personal values as you progress through the book.

Inner Compass, a Poem

Navigating across the ocean blue,
I hold an inner compass wonderfully true.

Holding me centered in all that I do.
Letting me Be for more than a minute or two.

Helping me see with clarity and vision.
Unlocking the key to trust my intuition.

My inner compass advantage,
No matter how the winds may change.

Allowing me to be the way,
To share my truth and light each day.

Required Self-Discovery

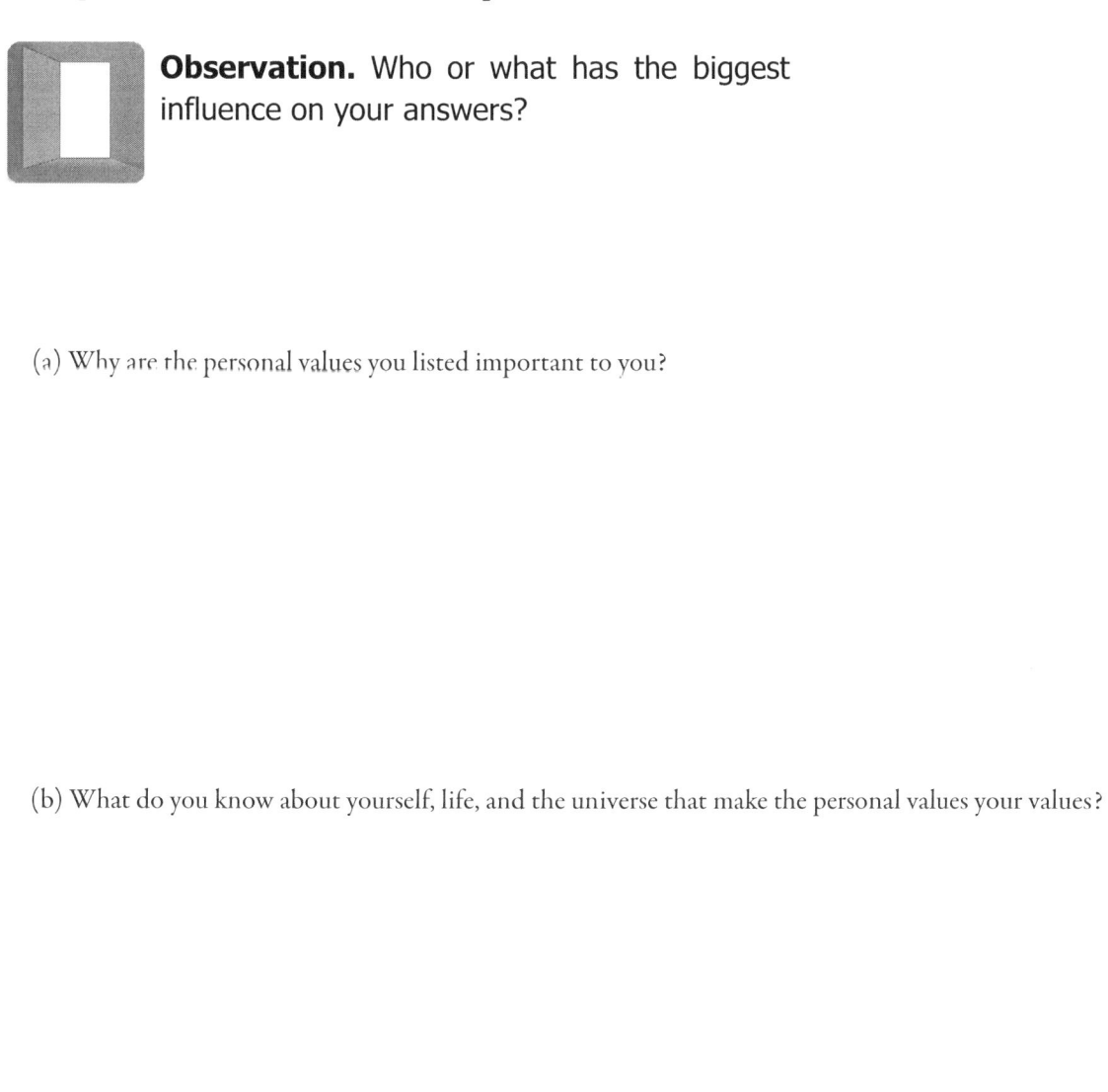

Observation. Who or what has the biggest influence on your answers?

(a) Why are the personal values you listed important to you?

(b) What do you know about yourself, life, and the universe that make the personal values your values?

(c) When you're under stress, where are your personal values?

Required Self-Discovery

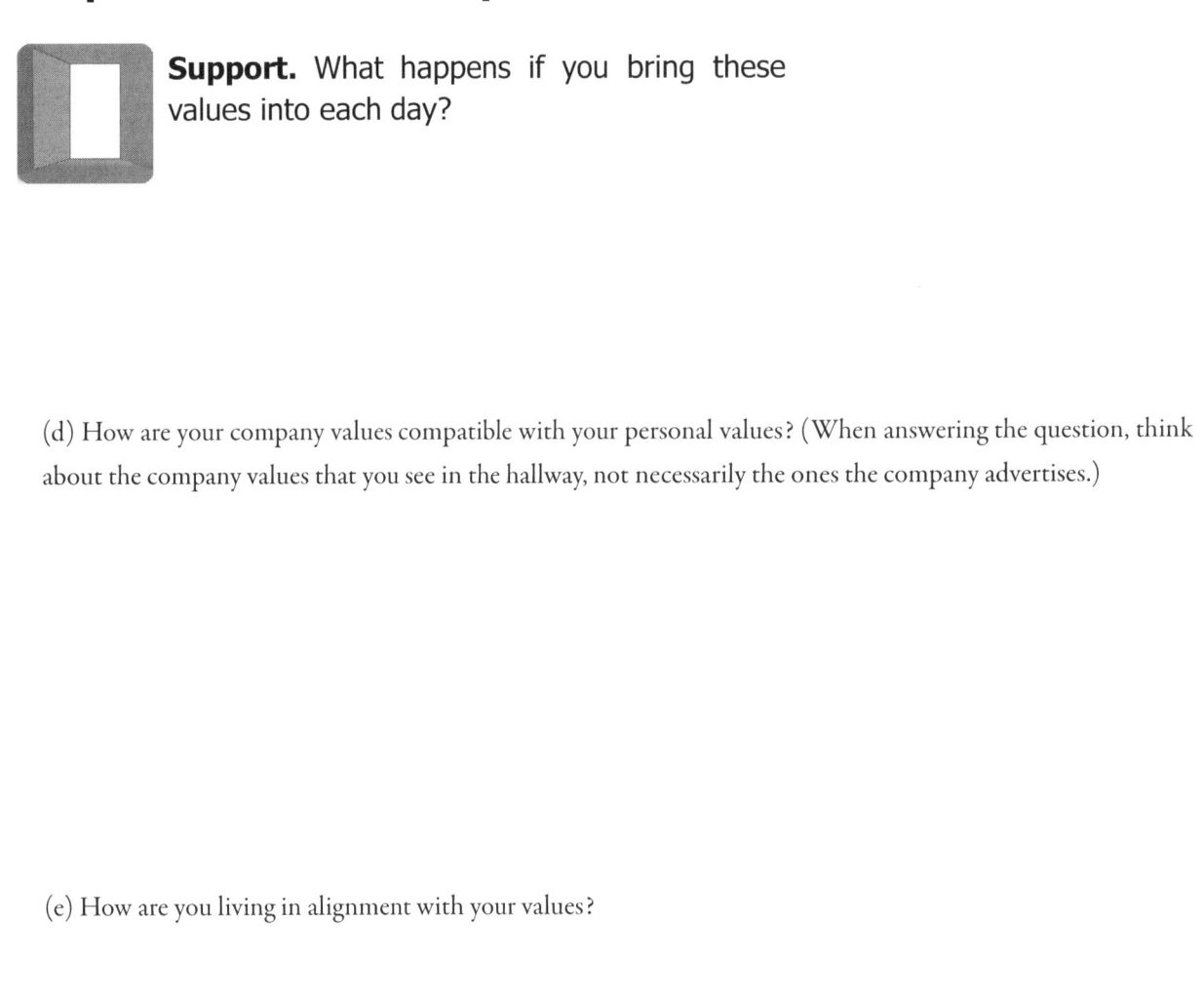

Support. What happens if you bring these values into each day?

(d) How are your company values compatible with your personal values? (When answering the question, think about the company values that you see in the hallway, not necessarily the ones the company advertises.)

(e) How are you living in alignment with your values?

Challenge yourself to get immediate feedback

Share your values with a close friend and ask them how you demonstrate your values.

Notes

Chapter 4

EXPERIENCES

If you can't explain it, you don't understand it well enough.
- Albert Einstein

In this chapter, you'll learn:

- What your experience has taught you
- How to view experiences as lessons learned

You are shifting from Preparation to early Action.

Finding Passion
Roadmap Across Stages of Change

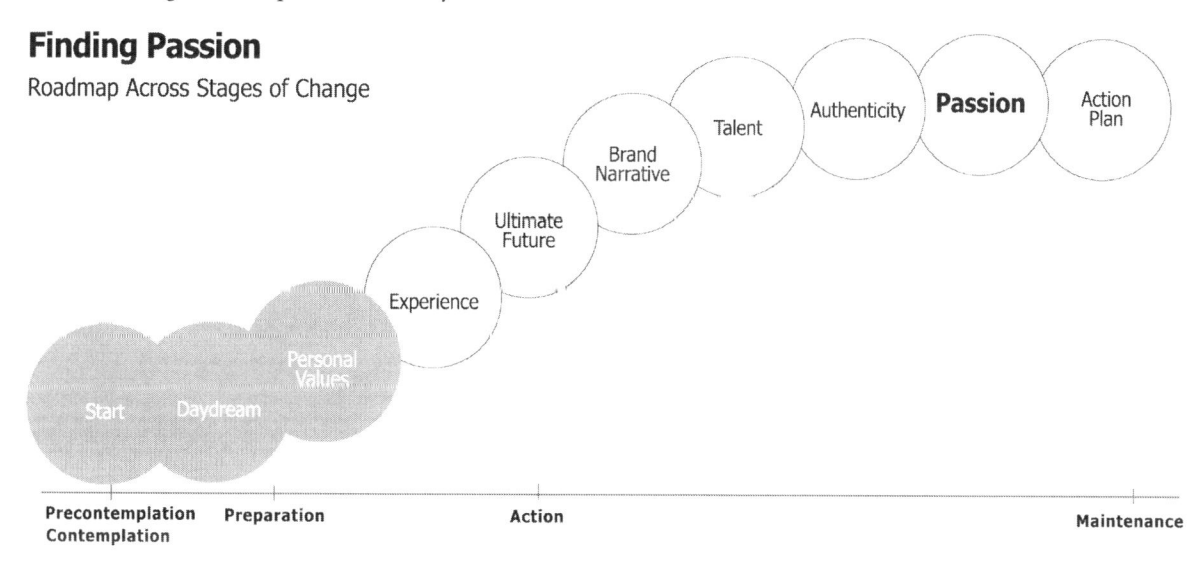

Figure 8. *Finding Passion* Roadmap, entering the Action stage of change.

Experiences

Our experience contains knowledge of times we've excelled and times we've learned some tough lessons. These experiences, both good and bad, give us reliable evidence of what works for us. With evidence comes a better understanding of the contributing factors that made our success possible. The evidence may uncover patterns that illuminate our Passion.

The next section is not a resume exercise. We're getting to the story behind the resume. Looking at your experience, what's the real story you wish everyone knew about you and your Passion?

What an Objective Observer Sees

In the weeks following my resignation, I'll never forgot one of the earlier sessions working with a professional coach to shape the future plan. My goal was to find the answer I'd been asking myself, "What do I really want?" I was looking for clues from my experience that would give me insight.

The coach questioned what kept me going through all my struggles. My answer was the relationships with my colleagues. I wanted to be strong for them, to ease the shared project pressure, and to make the work less serious. It was the people-side of motivating and building strong teams that was most rewarding to me.

The coach was neutral and helped me see options that I had overlooked, especially career ideas I had already dismissed. The first pattern she observed was a strong theme of teaching, motivating, and coaching. She heard my responses and saw a match across my experience, accomplishments, and resume details.

This observation got me thinking. I had taught continuing education for several summers, had earned an award as an internal performance coach, and had been curious about exploring professional coaching.

Then I remembered. I had expressed interest in delivering face-to-face coaching earlier that year within the firm. I had forgotten that I had already been considering professional coaching. Our local office didn't provide that service, so I would have been primarily working with, and reporting to, a team across the country. After some discussion both my partner and I recognized the idea wasn't feasible if I wanted to remain in my local office without moving to Halifax, but now this option was open again.

When we wrapped up the coaching call, I was exhilarated at the thought. Becoming a professional coach would enable me to live according to my personal values. Could this be my next career?

Excelling at Work | Exercise 4-1

Take a walk down memory lane as you focus on highlights from your career experience.

Preparation

- Grab a copy of your resume or bio for reference only.

- Use your investigator hat. Your role is to see what your resume says and what is hidden.

- Keep your eyes open for clues for finding your Passion. These clues will be themes that repeat themselves-- observations about where you've spent your energy and which of your major accomplishments still make you smile.

- Don't over-think the next exercises. Write the first answers that come to mind. Be efficient in passing through each question briskly.

- Grab a partner or someone who knows you through your previous jobs. Bounce ideas off this person as you answer the questions on the following pages.

Instructions

(1) Answer the questions in Exercise 4-1.

(2) Use the Notes section to sketch out keywords, observations, and important facts about what you do well.

Note: You may consider looking at any other sources for your experiences such as reference letters and recommendations from others.

Excelling at Work | Exercise 4-1

(a) Viewing your resume or bio, what makes you smile?

(b) In what category of work have you received recognition? Why?

(c) Considering your answer in Question b, what would you say are your talents?

Required Self-Discovery

Patterns. Name 1-2 things you've already been passionate about?

Notes

Learning Lessons | Exercise 4-2

Now, turn to the times you learned something about yourself, your work, and your career.

Preparation

- Continue keeping a copy of your resume or bio handy.

- Use your investigator hat. Your role is to see what your resume says and focus deeply on what is hidden.

- Continue as you did in the previous exercise, only with added vulnerability to see the truth. If feelings stir when you read the questions, this means you are tapping into a lesson. Try to listen for what your body is telling you.

- Continue working with a partner if you choose.

Instructions

(1) Answer the questions in Exercise 4-2.

(2) Use the Notes section to sketch out keywords, observations, and important facts to express what's important to consider in understanding your Passion.

Learning Lessons | Exercise 4-2

(a) Under what circumstances, if ever, did you struggle in your career?

(b) When you struggled, what was the cost to you?

(c) What feedback, in areas where you struggled, have you received that you haven't addressed yet? Describe the feedback below.

(d) What's preventing you from addressing the feedback?

Learning Lessons | Exercise 4-2

(e) What's the one thing, if anything, you're taking a stand on so that the lesson learned never repeats again?

(f) What experiences on your resume, if any, do you find difficult to explain?

(g) Where did you sugarcoat your experience on your resume? Why?

Required Self-Discovery

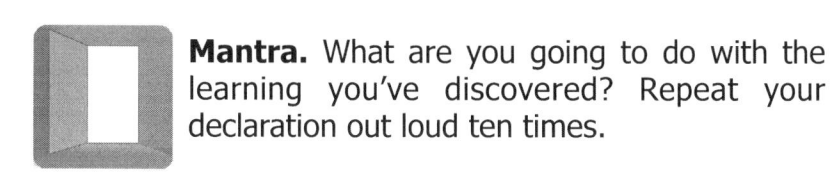

Mantra. What are you going to do with the learning you've discovered? Repeat your declaration out loud ten times.

(a) Are there any patterns you're starting to notice within your answers?

(b) What lessons, if any, have you come across in your career more than once?

Notes

Notes

Chapter 5

ULTIMATE FUTURE

When work, commitment, and pleasure all become one and you reach that deep well where passion lives, nothing is impossible.
- Unknown

In this chapter, you'll learn:

- How to gain clarity by defining the destination

- How symbols can support your Passion

You are in the Action stage and may be starting to change your behaviors.

Finding Passion
Roadmap Across Stages of Change

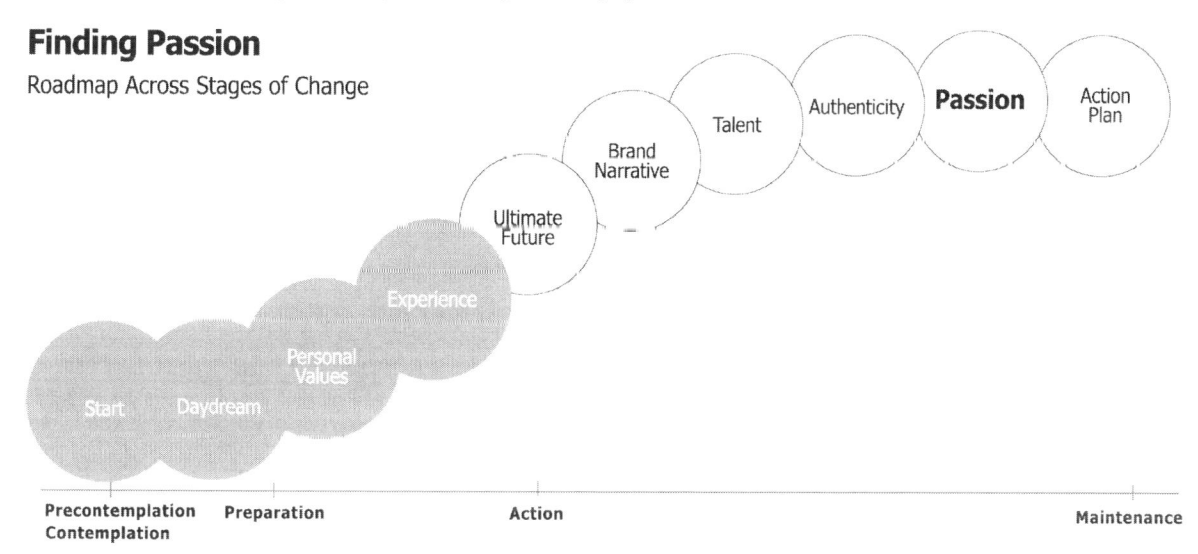

Figure 9. *Finding Passion* Roadmap, continuing within the Action stage of change.

Ultimate Future

The next section takes the previous answers one step deeper. Considering what you're discovering about personal values and experiences, you're going to tap into creativity to visualize an Ultimate Future.

Just as it sounds, an Ultimate Future is the outcome you're aspiring to. It's the big idea for the legacy you want to leave in life. It's a dream that once it comes true, you'll know you've made it.

This chapter marks our midpoint for *Finding Passion*. We're peeling the onion, layer by layer with our thinking, after years of operating in a particular mode. Now it's time to work toward what we truly want.

Living My Ultimate Future

Since I studied journalism, marketing, and visual communications in college, I had a faint picture of someday designing my own magazine. The magazine would be inspiring and be filled with practical ideas for living, clarifying, and organizing your life.

I knew that whatever I did for a living, it should involve creativity and be something I could show for my effort, something tangible. My first job as a graphic designer was compatible with this vision. However, as my roles got more technical and later more managerial, I grew further away from producing a tangible product.

I'm still attracted to this vision, sometimes simplifying it to "being an author." What was it about using my creativity and designing something that inspires others? How has this idea, first conceived more than twenty years ago, influenced me to write the workbook for you?

Your Ultimate Future | Exercise 5-1

This exercise is deliberate in working backward from what you can determine about your Ultimate Future to help you define your Passion later in Chapter 9.

Preparation

- Clear your mind of distractions; Sit in a creative place or quiet setting. Close your eyes for ten seconds, and picture the image you wrote on page 8.

- Ignore the critic in your mind that says the big idea can't be done. Today, you're going to stay in positive land where anything is possible.

- Continue to suspend your thoughts about how you'll get there.

- Take breaks frequently and reread your answers. The iterative nature of the exercise is much like peeling the onion of your understanding.

- Assume you have no constraints—money, time, availability of resources, or fear.

Instructions

(1) Ease into the next series of questions. Answer what you can.

(2) Use the Notes section, if needed.

Your Ultimate Future | Exercise 5-1

(a) The emotions I'm feeling right now when thinking about an Ultimate Future are:

(b) My Ultimate Future means I've achieved:

(c) I envision a future where:

Your Ultimate Future | Exercise 5-1

(d) I'm committed to the possibility of:

(e) To obtain my Ultimate Future, I'm committed to giving up:

(f) _____ is what I need to learn for my Ultimate Future.

Your Ultimate Future | Exercise 5-1

(g) What is your Ultimate Future?

(h) What types of skills might you need in your Ultimate Future?

Symbols

The values within your inner compass may be evident in reoccurring symbols and imagery around you. These totems represent values, qualities, and desires you hold most important. Putting these symbols where you can see them inspires and reminds you of what's important, much as a good luck charm does.

For example, my symbol is a circle. Circles remind me of symmetry, balance, and the connectedness of a single line that is complete. I enjoy looking at circles, as well as drawing them, especially creating hand-drawn Spirographs. Since I was little, circles have been speaking to me and making me feel at peace.

Your Symbols | Exercise 5-2

The next short exercise is designed to reveal whether symbols can strengthen the commitment to your Ultimate Future. Is the symbol itself the object of your Passion?

Preparation

- Spend a few moments thinking about images, doodles, and shapes you're attracted to.
- If you feel inspired to sketch, grab something to draw with.

Instructions

(1) Answer the following questions in Exercise 5-2.

(2) For fun, decorate the page with your symbols.

Your Symbols | Exercise 5-2

(a) What symbols seem to show up frequently in your life?

(b) Consider bringing symbols into your environment where you can see them. What would happen?

(c) Draw or paste your symbols on this page.

Required Self-Discovery

Accelerate. What's a simple step you could do to bring your Ultimate Future forward?

(a) What's shifted in your thinking since you started this workbook?

Notes

Pause

You've reached the midpoint. Take a moment to recognize your effort.

- **Getting Started.** You've taken action to move forward.

- **Daydream.** You've allowed yourself to remember your dreams.

- **Personal Values.** You've started to identify personal values to guide you forward.

- **Experience.** You've reminded yourself what you're capable of and what you've learned.

- **Ultimate Future.** You've shared your big dreams.

Next, you'll work through three more chapters before you define your Passion. You're getting closer with each passing day to living the life you want. This Passion of yours may be much larger than what you currently do.

Required Self-Discovery

Celebrate. If there is one thing you're most proud so far, what is it?

Notes

Chapter 6

PERSONAL BRAND AND NARRATIVE

It's not what you achieve, it's what you overcome. That's what defines your career.
- Carlton Fisk, Baseball Hall of Famer

In this chapter, you'll learn:

- To express a personal brand statement
- Ways to practice sharing your Passion
- The secret to your narrative

You are in the Action stage of personal change and continuing to modify your behaviors.

Finding Passion
Roadmap Across Stages of Change

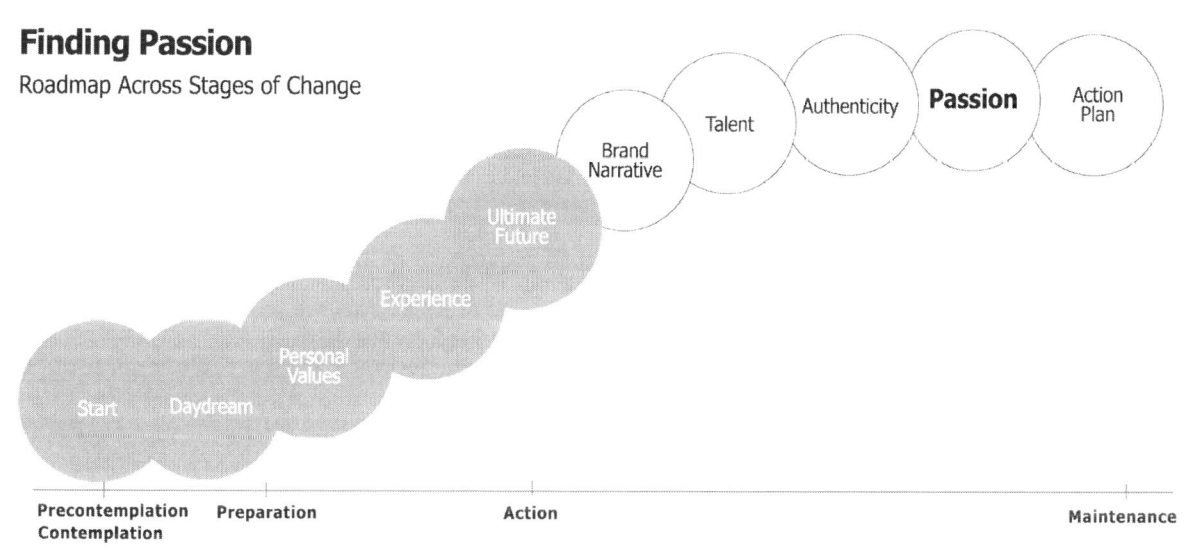

Figure 10. *Finding Passion* Roadmap, continuing to modify behavior within the Action stage.

Personal Brand and Narrative

What better way to begin an Ultimate Future than to tell others about it? Success depends on many factors, but one factor within your control is having the help of supporters, influencers, and mentors to realize your vision. They can be advocates, clients, friends and family, advisors, and people of influence who support you in getting your message out there. Let's review two helpers you can use to convey your message to get supporters on board.

Personal Brand

Personal brand is the "what you're known for." Tom Peters, author and business consultant, describes it as "your promise to the marketplace and the world." A personal brand reflects what you do and how you show up in life. It's a statement answering what you're best at (value), the people you serve, your audience, and your unique selling proposition (USP).

Your personal brand is the sum of your narratives. It conveys the essence of your personality and can be catchy, fun, and easy to remember.

Narrative

Narrative is the story that explains exactly how your past fits with the present. The narrative depicts your past from the perspective of how events led you to where you are today. This is a story only you can tell, and it's not the resume but the story behind the resume. The narrative you create can be as short as one or two sentences and will change often as the personal brand evolves.

No matter what your Passion, both the personal brand and narrative will be valuable strategies that you'll need moving forward.

A Statement That Inspires Me

Sharing my inner light, I coach others to bring alignment to their greater purpose.

My personal brand means I'm sharing my story. Through sharing and coaching, I help others find their greater purpose and Passion.

If I show up to every day with this statement in mind, I am mindful and authentic. The statement inspires me to bring forward the best of myself as I serve others.

Your Personal Brand | Exercise 6-1

If personal values are those internal drivers for how we think and behave, then a personal brand represents what others consistently see. Exercise 6-1 provides guidance for developing your personal brand.

Preparation

- Review Chapter 1, "Getting Started," before beginning this exercise. Review whether there any techniques for self-reflection that you have yet to experiment with.

- While there is no set formula for developing a personal brand, there are common bits of information conveyed in a personal brand. Read the sample statements for some ideas:

    - **Consultant.** I problem solve, strategize, and articulate the complex challenges of clients, building operational controls and processes that reduce impacts to running and growing their business vision.

    - **Business owner.** I provide sensible, innovative and scalable solutions by advising and being advised by my clients, deeply understanding their vision and offering the necessary expertise that propels their business and ours into a trusted and successful partnership.

    - **Musician.** I am a passionate, creative and inspirational musician who brings energy, discipline and direction to open-minded, engaged, and curious audiences in order to create a memorable auditory experience that enriches their lives.

- Be vulnerable. Relax, and accept that there are no wrong answers.

- Take your time with the exercise. Play around with word choice and order.

Instructions

(1) Complete Exercise 6-1. Experiment with your personal brand statement. This is a draft version, so leave energy to revise it later.

(2) When ready, continue onto Exercise 6-2.

Your Personal Brand | Exercise 6-1

(a) What makes you stand apart? What is your best characteristic?

(b) What value do you provide with your work?

(c) Whom do you do it for?

Your Personal Brand | Exercise 6-1

(d) Create your personal brand statement below.

(e) How are your personal values reflected in your brand? What can make your brand stronger?

Your Narrative | Exercise 6-2

Exercise 6-2 requires you to talk out loud when answering the questions asked. Bring your inner compass and symbols with you when answering these questions.

Preparation

- Be vulnerable. Relax, and accept that there are no wrong answers.

- Grab a partner to play out the scenario on the next page. Bounce ideas off your partner as you answer the questions on the following pages.

- Pretend you just met a person of influence who's interested in hearing more about you. Practice by test-driving your story.

- Consider recording this exchange on a voice recording.

Instructions

(1) Practice Exercise 6-2. The person of influence is asking the questions of you.

(2) Once you've practiced the exercise, read on to "The Secret to Your Narrative." Repeat the exercise.

(3) Use your notes to recall your observations, including how your posture and energy levels may play a factor.

Your Narrative | Exercise 6-2

(a) "...So, what do you do?"

(b) "How interesting. But how does a person who was a [your previous role] become a [your new role]?"

(c) "Our mutual friend said you had a big idea that I'd be interested in. What is it?"

(d) "I'd really like to help you. What do you need from me?"

The Secret to Your Narrative

Now that you've completed this walk-through, here's a secret. Your narrative, despite what people may say, is not about selling yourself to others. It's about sharing your Passion!

When you smile and start talking with conviction, you'll have won half the battle at conveying that idea to others. Using your inner compass, repeat this exercise, adding to or revising your responses for Exercise 6-2.

> **My New Personal Brand in Action**
>
> My personal brand inspired me, and now I needed to practice talking about my experience when I meet others. This part is harder than coming up with the statement itself.
>
> I attended a networking luncheon shortly after I drafted my revised brand, and it was my first opportunity to test it. That morning, I decided that that the biggest thing I could do was just be myself. I was going to show up as me.
>
> The practice was easier than I thought.
>
> I sat next to women who were also new to the meeting (interconnectedness is everywhere), and I introduced myself. My personal values gave me strength to say what came naturally and to be curious about others. I felt open and full of light.
>
> A new acquaintance commented that I was glowing when I talked about starting my new career. I was so flattered. Ironically, I didn't have a job yet. I was just starting to look at the profession of coaching and to evaluate certification programs. The energy coming from my story was tangible. I knew I was on the right track.

Required Self-Discovery

(a) What else do you need to prepare your narrative?

(b) How confident are you with speaking your narrative?

(c) How are you managing the difficult questions?

Challenge yourself to practice your narrative

Take advantage of opportunities to practice your narrative. The next time you run into someone new who asks, "Exactly what do you do," test out your answer using your personal values to support you.

Notes

Notes

Chapter 7

TALENTS

Every man has his own vocation, talent is the call.
- Ralph Waldo Emerson

In this chapter, you'll learn:

- How to recognize your talents

- How to identify gaps between your current skills and your Ultimate Future skills

- Which areas to focus on for your personal development within your action plan

You are in the Action stage and continuing to change behaviors.

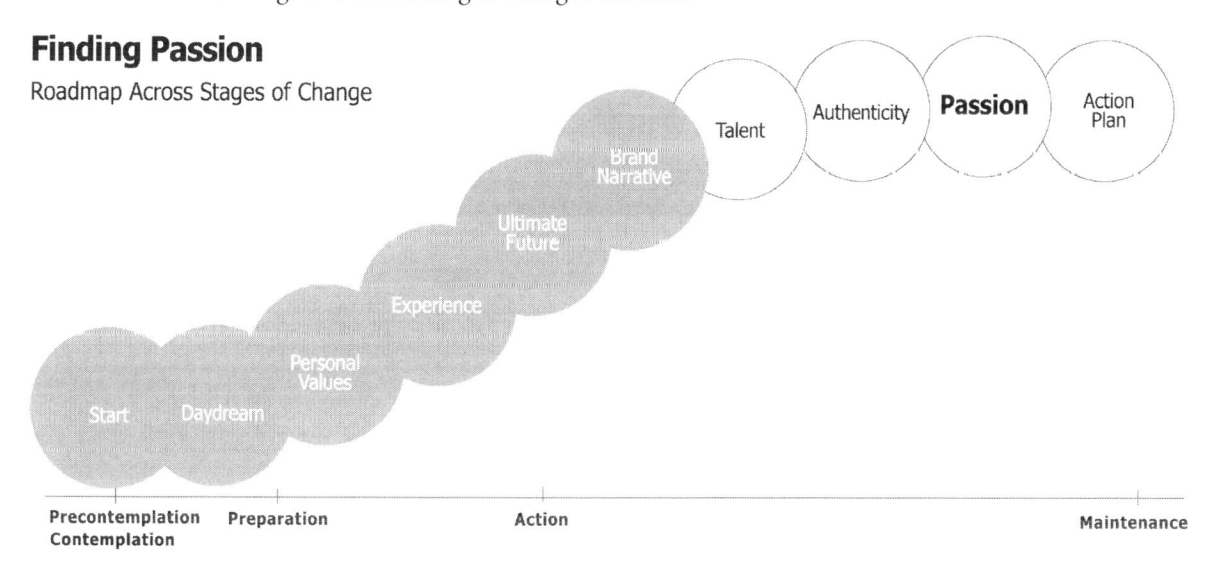

Figure 11. *Finding Passion* Roadmap, identifying shifts in behavior within the Action stage.

Talents

A talent can be inherent in how we operate, work, and create. It's always there with us consistently. Whether we're at work, at home, or on vacation, our talent makes challenges in life seem easy. As personal values establish our foundation, talent propels our effort and brings us closer to our Passion.

Think about what comes naturally and effortlessly to you even if you can't really explain why. You'll compare talents to skills and strengths to help you determine what's needed for your Ultimate Future. Your findings will help to build the personal development area of the action plan developed later in Chapter 10.

- **Skills.** Skills are abilities that you have learned, studied, and improved. Typing is a skill; however, having a gift for expression and analogy may be the talent.

- **Strengths.** Strengths include skills that you have mastered through practice and discipline. Using the typing example, you may be able to type (skill); however, typing 60 word per minute with no mistakes would be a strength.

> ### Building Blocks
>
> Although it may feel at times that we start from scratch when we change jobs or positions, we're actually working from a broad set of building blocks. My previous experience has somehow been exactly what I needed. Combined with my natural talents, developing new skills is far from starting from scratch. Both experience and talent join to help me gain new skills, develop strengths, or allow my talent to shine even more.

Prepare for your talent and existing skill-set to be a part of the Passion you'll define in Chapter 9.

Talent and Skills Builder | Exercise 7

Identify your natural talents to further propel you toward finding your Passion. Identify skills needed and use your talent list to provide the building blocks to work from.

Preparation

- Prepare for this exercise by thinking back to the times when you expended effort that seemed easy.

- Recall times when others said they wished they could do something as easily as you.

- For additional clues, look at the tools, materials, and workspace around you. They might reveal something about your working style and natural tendencies when at work.

Instructions

(1) At the top of the worksheet, name three talents.

(2) In Column 1, list the skills you have today that you feel are important to use moving forward.

(3) Shift your focus to your Ultimate Future. Begin listing future skills fitting that profile. If you're unsure of what to list here without conducting research, make a note for adding a brainstorming activity as part of Exercise 10, Developing an Action Plan.

(4) From Column 1, circle and draw an arrow to Column 2 for any skill that needs strengthening for your future. Within the Action Required column, write a specific action for developing this skill.

(5) In the Ultimate Future column, circle any skills that you don't yet possess or don't possess to the strength desired. Draw an arrow from Column 3 to Column 2. Write down a short-term action for developing this skill in Column 2. As a guide, set Column 2 actions within a four- to six-month timeframe.

(6) Cross check with your previous answers for clues:

- **Page 34.** Review Exercise 4-1 (c), Excelling at Work.

- **Page 37.** Review Exercise 4-2 (d), Learning Lessons.

- **Page 48.** Review Exercise 5-1 (h), Ultimate Future.

- **Page 60.** Review Exercise 6-1 and your personal brand for ideas.

Note: There are numerous ways to perform the exercise. The next page displays a completed sample from my personal work to guide you. You may choose any of the above, or experiment with what you feel works best for you. Your goal is to shake down the existing and future skills you need.

Talent and Skills Builder | Exercise 7 | Example

Table 2. My Talent and Skills Builder (Example)

TALENT AND SKILL BUILDER
Attention to detail, drive, and motivating others

EXISTING SKILLS	ACTION REQUIRED	ULTIMATE FUTURE SKILLS
Self-awareness	Be open to feedback, and seeking two-way dialogue	Self-awareness and emotional intelligence
Sensibility, vulnerability	Reduce rules, labels that confine relationships	Centered-self, without boundaries or labels
Managing complexity; rigor	Adjust "right way" and black/white thinking; practice kindness to self	Open minded, always learning
Self-reliance	Accentuate strength in character with daily courage	Flexible (opposite of being attached to outcomes)
Attention to detail	Keep focused on the long view; not tied to every detail	Inner peace, mindfulness, meditation in daily rituals
Compassion	Seek permission more from others; face truths together	Brutally honest in relationships
Creative	Let loose to work when creativity strikes; have fun	Balancing energy rather than time
Project management and discipline	Shift from outcome-oriented to empowering others	Storytelling
High expectations and standards	Watch for perfectionist tendencies	Able to ask and accept the help of others
	Create accountability partners to help me improve	Increased accountability for my actions, words
	Practice daily gratitude and express feelings more often	Gratitude
	Continue daily rituals to stay balanced	

Talent and Skills Builder | Exercise 7

TALENT AND SKILLS BUILDER

EXISTING SKILLS	ACTION REQUIRED	ULTIMATE FUTURE SKILLS

Required Self-Discovery

(a) How will talent play a part in expressing your Passion?

(b) What fears came to mind when you completed the Ultimate Future skills column?

(c) From what you know today, who are the key people you need to help you develop the Ultimate Future skills?

Embrace your talent

Celebrate the little things that you like to do. Appreciate in the moment when you're using your talent as well as the tools and people helping you.

Notes

Chapter 8

AUTHENTICITY

When your values, intention, and behavior are in alignment, there can be no regret.
- Jessica Manca

In this chapter, you'll learn:

- How to assess values-beliefs-intention alignment to gauge your authenticity

- How vulnerability expands your perception

You are in the Action stage and continuing to change behaviors.

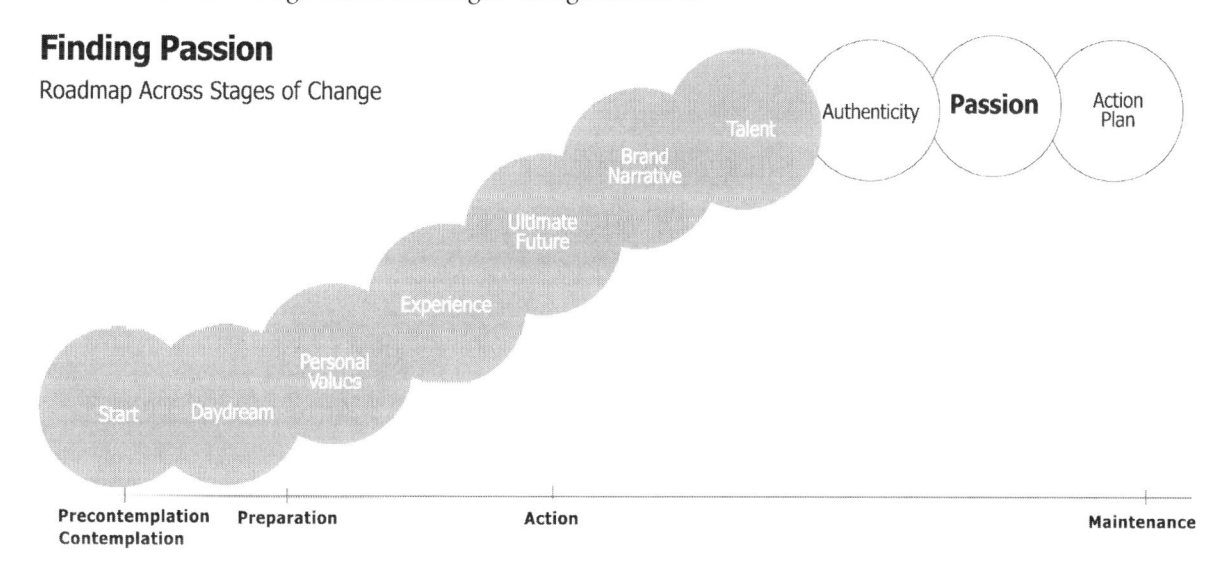

Figure 12. *Finding Passion* Roadmap, continuing in the Action stage of change toward defining Passion.

Authenticity

In our lives, we play many diverse roles. Different shades of ourselves may emerge within different contexts. We're more serious at work than at home. We're more playful at home than at work. However, at the core, it's still me or you. Despite our different roles, there's a consistency among the qualities that emerge. If, instead, we feel as if we're wearing a mask to pretend to be something we're not (especially at work), we probably are not being genuine.

You now must pass one major gate to test everything you've been working on. You must make sure that blind spots and beliefs you hold about yourself aren't the barriers that prevent you from realizing your Ultimate Future and Passion.

When you think of living an authentic life, what does this mean? Authenticity is being true to who you are. It means you're genuine and real. You're not pretending. You believe what you say and have high integrity for your commitments to others and yourself.

Values-Beliefs-Intentions Alignment

Leveraging all of your work in defining your personal values, you're now going to map out how to bring those values forward every day. This aspect of self-discovery work may be the most powerful described in this book. Here's what to look for when it comes to alignment of values, beliefs, and intentions.

- **Beliefs**. A belief is a statement you know to be true about the world or yourself. Beliefs influence you, often in ways you can't directly see. Beliefs form a world view, influencing you and sometimes holding you back. When you selected your personal values, there was a strong belief which connected those words to meaning in your life.

- **Intention**. Beliefs influence intention or the premeditated outcome you're working toward. Intentions may be general, as in, "I want to have a good day today," or more specific, as in, "I commit to sticking to priorities and not getting distracted by other tasks."

- **Alignment**. When the three areas of values, beliefs, and intentions align, there's a far better chance for success. Habits develop more naturally, and you have less of that feeling of expending a lot of effort to get little results. While alignment doesn't guarantee you won't face obstacles, it does support learning and being flexible when those obstacles come in front of you.

- **Old beliefs.** An intention tied to an old belief shows up in your life as self-sabotage. What this means is you're saying one thing (such as a new intention) while your behavior suggests the opposite (influenced by your old beliefs). Uncovering inconsistencies here can really unlock your potential.

To fully illustrate this point, here's an example. A woman person wants to keep fit and increase her level of healthiness. She changes her diet, she exercises, and gets plenty of rest, only the habit doesn't fully form or last long. She holds an old belief and story that she can never be fit. The old belief is the saboteur and is the key piece that needs to shift in order for her to make lasting change. She's got the determination and motivation to change yet she needs to replace the old belief with a newer one that works together with her intention and behavior.

You've worked through your personal values, and know your intention is to answer, "What do I really want?" Start thinking about old beliefs that come to mind and that may need to shift, given where you are on your journey. You might recognize old beliefs that start off like this: "I've always been…" or "I never…" Both are strong declarations to either always be or never be a certain way. Do these declarations get in the way of the change you want?

Masking My Feelings with Armor

The masks I wore when I hid my emotions, my stress, and guilt were like armor, protecting me from harm. The armor shielded the truth that I needed to take a hard look at making personal changes. Here's how my authenticity came through, both internally and externally, based on my reflections and performance feedback I received.

INTERNALLY	EXTERNALLY
Felt like an impostor	Came across as keen
Worked to make good impressions	Made others aware of personal success
Hid mistakes and the amount of effort used	Seemed very agreeable
Lost my voice; ability to make decisions	Worked to control situations or outcomes
Clothes felt like an actor's wardrobe	Focused on work at all times
Looked for cues before saying the "right" or "best" answer	Seemed unnecessarily assertive, not always a team player

I became obsessed with getting the promotion. All my behaviors stemmed from that intention. Like an actor, I took on the role I thought I should play. You've heard the expression, "Fake it 'til you make it?" What once was a motto now makes me shudder.

I couldn't have been further from my personal values of truth, interconnectedness, and distillment. I wasn't truthful, kept feelings bottled up, and tried to control the situation. Keeping up the charade was exhausting. No wonder I felt sick to my stomach when I got up for work in the morning.

The job was stressful, but my less-than-authentic approach to it only made matters worse. Getting back to the true me underneath was going to take time. It would also require permission to trust my intuition and listen to the signals my body was sending me.

Authenticity Assessment | Exercise 8-1

The next page contains an assessment for measuring your authenticity. The short quiz is not comprehensive and is intended as a gauge for your overall level of authenticity.

Preparation

- Avoid encrypting the truth with your answers.
- Be accepting of the results you find, even if they vary from what you expect.
- Be honest with yourself.

Instructions

(1) Rate the following listed in Exercise 8-1 on a scale from 0–10.

(2) Add up your score.

(3) Use your notes to confess your truths.

Authenticity Assessment | Exercise 8-1

Table 3. Authenticity Assessment and Rating Scale

```
0                         5                        10
|---|---|---|---|---|---|---|---|---|---|
  Disagree            Sometimes              Agree
```

AUTHENTICITY ASSESSMENT

STATEMENT	RATING
I show up in life authentically. I'm being myself.	
I have true relationships and meaningful connections with everyone in my life and at work.	
I'm happy with my actions, regardless of what others think.	
I'm transparent with my behavior; There's no hidden agenda with me.	
I'm content to be far away from mind games, office politics, or gossip.	
I'm OK with openly admitting my mistakes to others.	
I make informed decisions on my own rather than decide based on what others want.	
I'm comfortable with voicing my opinion even when it's not a popular view.	
I'm open to feedback and can take it with kindness.	
TOTAL SCORE	

Authenticity Assessment | Exercise 8-1 | Scoring Results

70+   **Strong Authenticity**

You're living authentically. Consistently, your responses reveal you've got authenticity well aligned with who you are.

Take a moment to acknowledge how your personal values support you in staying true to who you are. You're going to soar through the following sections.

27 to 69   **Some Authenticity**

There's work to do. By now, you might be seeing where you're wearing a mask. There's a reason this mask developed. You needed it (for better or worse). Maybe now is a time to shed the layers between you and authentic connections with others?

How can you take the results from this assessment and become the person you aspire to be? In the next section, pay close attention to beliefs you hold that need to shift, and create new ones that better align with your current needs. Use the notes section to reflect upon your findings.

0 to 27   **Low Authenticity**

You might consider additional coaching and exercises to assist you in this area. See Appendix - Maintenance Program.

Similar to the results for the 27–69 range but to a larger degree, your results may indicate relationships are suffering with others. Most likely, the relationship you have with yourself is at risk of constant conflict. To move forward, you'll need to make a commitment to yourself to be genuine.

Take the next section slowly, and be forgiving of yourself. You're on your way to resolving the situation, which means you'll be on the other side of this soon. Use the notes section to reflect upon your findings.

Vulnerability

Vulnerability is a part of the human condition that helps us understand we're not so different in our experiences. Each time we're vulnerable, we expand our perception, and, as in this book, our self-awareness. Being vulnerable is not easy to do; however, the more you can express your vulnerability around sensitive experiences and fears, the more powerfully your message comes through.

Being vulnerable moves you forward

Take a moment to acknowledge how you've demonstrated vulnerability thus far. By committing to finding your Passion, you've been:

- **Open**. Willing to answer difficult questions about yourself.

- **Inquisitive**. Careful to understand yourself for the emotions stirred, the memories revisited and the things that are in your mind that you're starting to write down, likely for the first time. You're letting these ideas out of their bottle.

- **Courageous**. Ready to let go of old thinking that got you here, and approaching each exercise with honesty to face your truth.

Daily Acts of Courage

Right now is a great time to take on a daily act of courage. Your mind is active and full of ideas towards the future you desire so put that energy to good use. Keep your momentum going by taking on the smallest of actions each day. All you need is to identify an activity, commit to doing it, and make it the first thing you tackle in your day. Why the first thing? So you kick-start your plan every day and not allow excuses or overthinking to get in the way.

After a few days or weeks of developing this habit, you'll have momentum to make change and start feeling better. Watch out for waiting until all conditions are in place before making change. If you hear yourself saying, "Well, as soon as…" then a daily act of courage might be just what you need to get started now with no waiting.

In the next exercise, continue expanding your perspective by looking at your values, beliefs, and intentions alignment.

Your Alignment | Exercise 8-2

Next, evaluate how you're expressing your personal values or whether you have some areas that need to shift.

Preparation

- Trust your intuition.
- Recall your personal values listed in your inner compass Exercise 3.

Instructions

(1) Upon reviewing and reflecting on your score, begin Exercise 8-2, Your Alignment.

(2) Recapture your personal values on the following pages in more detail. Feel free to modify them if your understanding of your values has changed since earlier in the workbook. You may decide to collapse two values into one, or expand a value by choosing a new word that resonates with you.

(3) Complete the personal value alignment for each value on a separate page. Using discoveries from the Exercise 8-1, Authenticity Assessment, map out your alignment for each value. Five pages have been provided for you. Should you need more space, use your notes.

(4) An example is provided as a guide.

Your Alignment | Exercise 8-2 | Example

Table 4. My Alignment (Example for truth value)

YOUR ALIGNMENT

PERSONAL VALUE	MY BELIEFS
Truth	You can't hide from truth. To see your truth, you must be vulnerable. Truth is found in both positive and negative experiences. I use my intuition in my personal life, but not at work. (Old)
MY INTENTION	NEW BELIEFS
I choose to speak my truth.	Listening to instincts is critical for me to be truthful and to be myself. There is no separation from the work "me" and the personal "me."

Your Alignment | Exercise 8-2

Table 5. Your Alignment Value #1

YOUR ALIGNMENT

PERSONAL VALUE	MY BELIEFS
MY INTENTION	NEW BELIEFS
I choose…	I will…

AUTHENTICITY

Your Alignment | Exercise 8-2

Table 6. Your Alignment Value #2

YOUR ALIGNMENT

PERSONAL VALUE	MY BELIEFS
MY INTENTION	NEW BELIEFS
I choose…	I will…

Your Alignment | Exercise 8-2

Table 7. Your Alignment Value #3

YOUR ALIGNMENT

PERSONAL VALUE	MY BELIEFS
MY INTENTION	NEW BELIEFS
I choose…	I will…

AUTHENTICITY

Your Alignment | Exercise 8-2

Table 8. Your Alignment Value #4

YOUR ALIGNMENT

PERSONAL VALUE	MY BELIEFS
MY INTENTION	NEW BELIEFS
I choose…	I will…

Your Alignment | Exercise 8-2

Table 9. Your Alignment Value #5

YOUR ALIGNMENT

PERSONAL VALUE	MY BELIEFS
MY INTENTION	NEW BELIEFS
I choose…	I will…

AUTHENTICITY

Required Self-Discovery

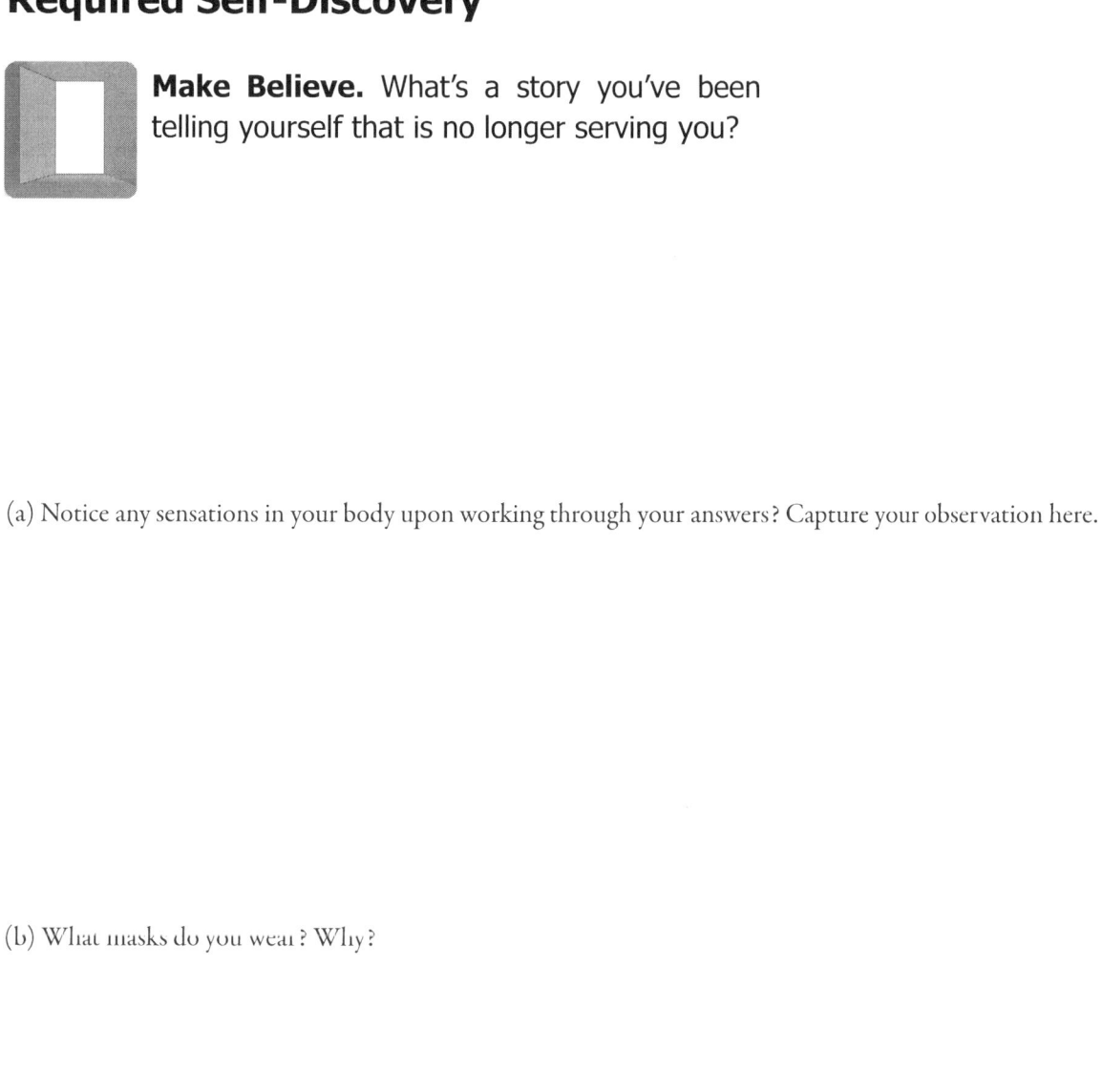

Make Believe. What's a story you've been telling yourself that is no longer serving you?

(a) Notice any sensations in your body upon working through your answers? Capture your observation here.

(b) What masks do you wear? Why?

(c) What beliefs, if any, need to shift?

Required Self-Discovery

(d) What's the most important change you need to make to become more authentic?

Challenge yourself to live in alignment

Bring your personal values more into your life, and reconsider the decisions you make which don't fall in alignment. Catch yourself when old beliefs show up, and replace them with new ones.

Notes

Chapter 9

PASSION

In the depth of winter, I finally learned that there was within me an invincible summer.
- Albert Camus, Nobel Prize Winner

In this chapter, you'll see:

- How much you've learned about your Passion
- The next steps to bringing Passion forward

You are in the Action stage and continue to change behaviors.

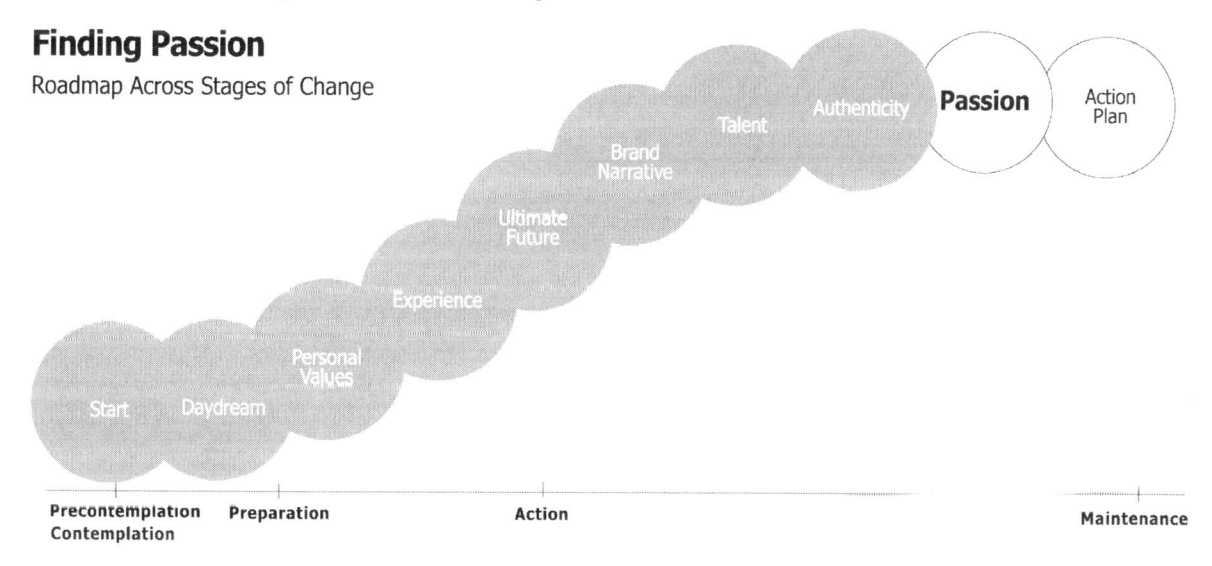

Figure 13. *Finding Passion* Roadmap, ready to define your Passion.

Passion

This is the answer you've been waiting for. What do you really want? Bringing all the tools together that you've learned on the journey, you can apply what you do know to shape your Passion.

Finding Passion

My Passion: To infuse others with light, to inspire essential change, and to illuminate the path of greater purpose.

When I think about my personal values, they are broad considerations helping me to live, see, and describe my Passion. These conditions translated into sharing stories and lessons (truth), building authentic relationships with honest communication (interconnectedness), and listening to find the the root cause that can hold someone back (essence).

Figure 14. My Passion pie chart.

With personal values as a base, there are other elements that bring out my best, including managing my energy, learning through ongoing self-awareness, and listening to my intuition often.

Identifying the elements helps me to be prepared to bring my Passion forward each day. If my Passion where a pie, these elements would be the ingredients. My Passion creates a fulfilling life for me. It means a life lived true to who I am that leads me to happiness.

Your Passion | Exercise 9

Let your Passion out in this exercise. Summarize what you're looking for in life, and what it takes to find fulfillment in your career. The goal remains that once you find Passion, the decisions you make in your career become easier because you're confident you're true to yourself.

Preparation

- Think about your picture of possibilities. Hold the image in your mind, take a deep breath, and begin.

- There are no wrong answers.

Instructions

(1) Answer the question, "What is Your Passion?"

(2) Repeat your personal values list below your Passion statement or description.

(3) Use the pie chart to identify the elements that need to be in place for your Passion.

(4) Put each element into a slice. Add more slices if you like.

(5) You can think of these slices as the criteria for making your Passion possible or even the criteria you must have for your next career or job opportunity. Refer to the items you mentioned in Exercise 2, Remembering Dreams.

Your Passion | Exercise 9

Today's date: _____

My Passion is to...

Your Passion | Exercise 9 | Passion Pie Chart

My Passion is made up of these pieces below

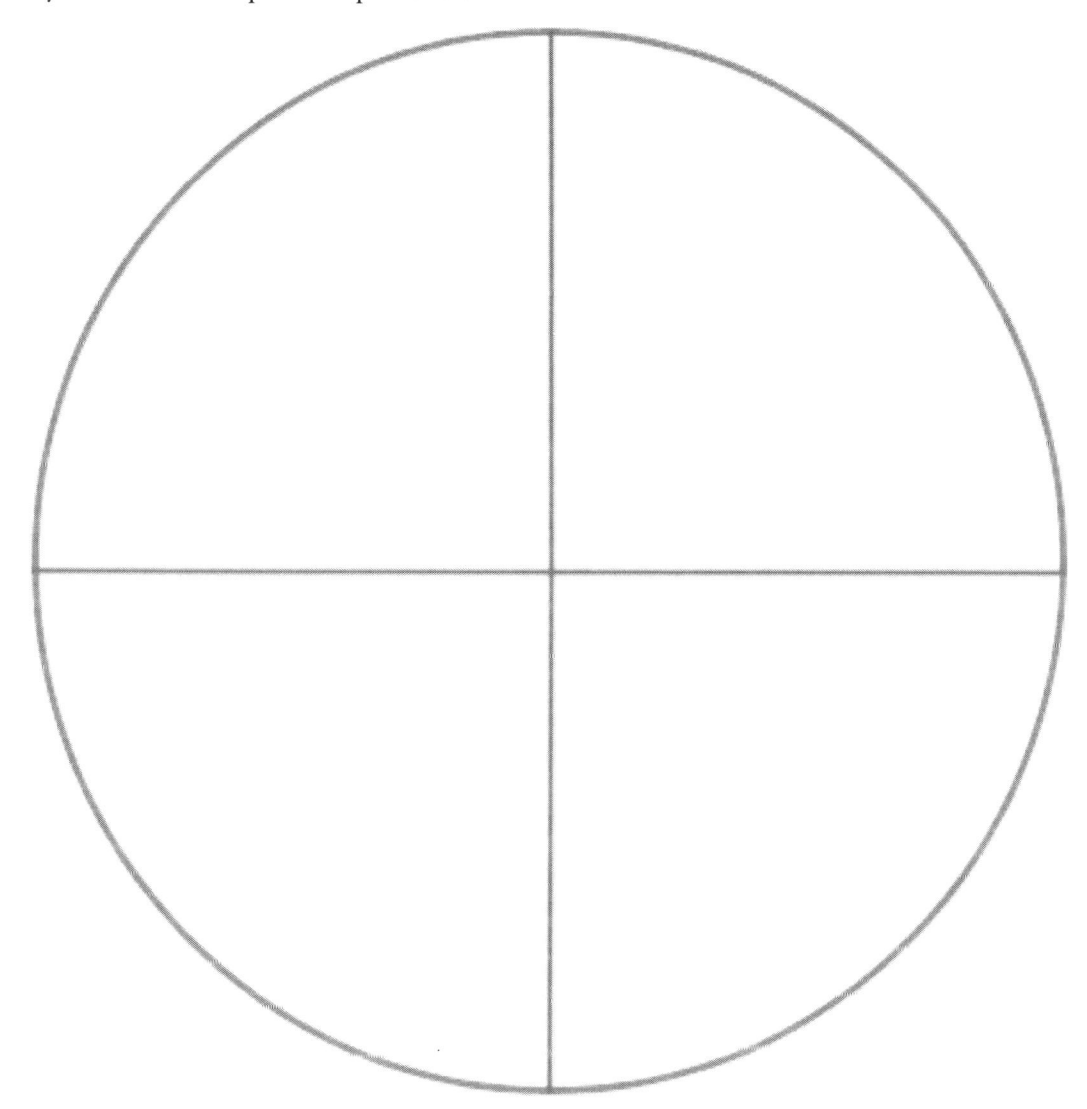

Figure 15. Your Passion pie chart.

Required Self-Discovery

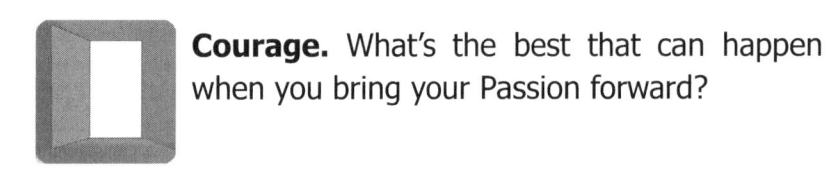

Courage. What's the best that can happen when you bring your Passion forward?

(a) What are you prepared to do about your career?

Challenge yourself to bring your Passion forward

For the next twenty days, take on the challenge of bringing your Passion forward. Dedicate five minutes at the start of every day when you're brushing your teeth in the morning or slipping on your shoes before you walk out the door to think about the various pieces of your Passion. It's up to you to keep this Passion alive, embrace it, and celebrate it each day. To strengthen your commitment, the final chapter helps you prepare your action plan.

Notes

Chapter 10

ACTION PLAN

We are what we repeatedly do. Excellence, therefore, is not an act but a habit.
- Aristotle

In this chapter, you'll learn:

- How to use an action plan framework to bring your Passion forward and face career crossroads

- Which areas to include in your action plan, focused on the "how"

- How to set action in place that brings your Ultimate Future and Passion one day closer

You are in the Action stage and continue to strengthen your commitment to follow your Passion.

Finding Passion
Roadmap Across Stages of Change

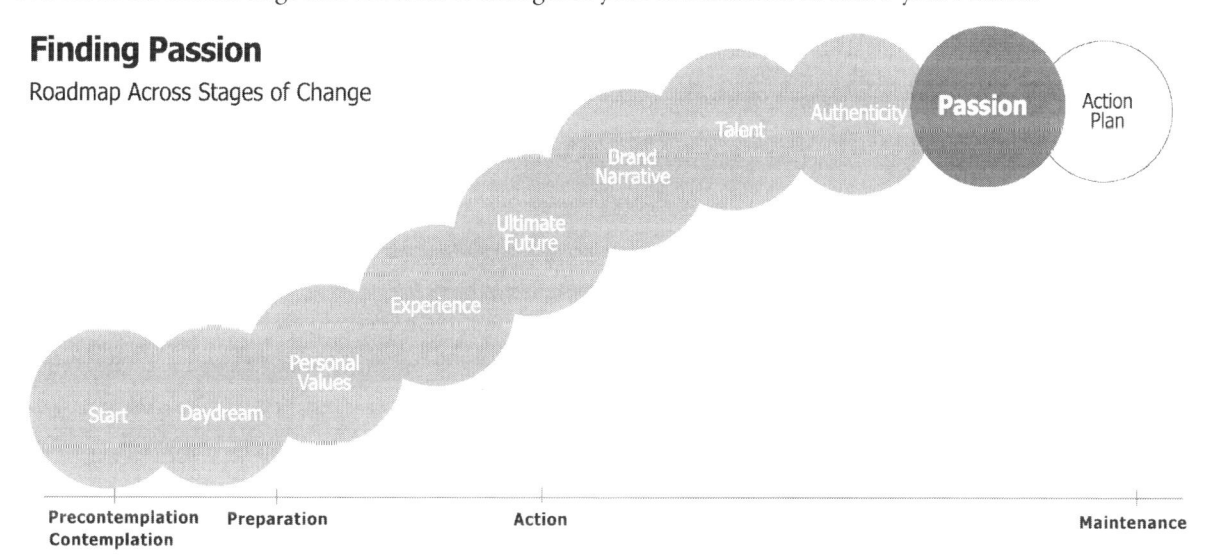

Precontemplation / Contemplation — Preparation — Action — Maintenance

Start · Daydream · Personal Values · Experience · Ultimate Future · Brand Narrative · Talent · Authenticity · **Passion** · Action Plan

Figure 16. *Finding Passion* Roadmap, deepening your commitment under the Action stage of change.

103

Action Plan

The next chapter lays out a plan to help you bring your Passion forward and assist you in making decisions about your career next steps. You can now take a serious look at "how" to bring your Passion to life. If you refer back to the outputs of the last nine chapters, the action plan can be effective at helping you come up with activities to support your goals.

If you haven't taken action thus far within your findings from the previous work or challenges, now is your opportunity. Your action plan will focus on bite-sized activities to get you started. As you experience small successes and momentum, you can update your action plan into larger views such as a ninety-day or one- or three-year plans.

Framework for action planning

For any plan, there are three areas to consider: scope, time, and costs. These areas interplay to form a sensible action plan that meets your timing and budgetary requirements.

For personal action planning, there's an additional component labeled, "Significance." I've discovered that plans can have great intentions and still fail. The purpose of adding significance to a particular activity or area of focus means you're defining what's in it for you. You're reminding yourself of the effect of remaining where you are rather than move forward. This step can help you confirm that each activity is working toward your overall goal.

Inputs to your action plan

As you prepare for the action plan, here are some suggested areas to include.

- **Stepping stones.** Name three small things you need now that require little effort and can begin immediately.

- **Inner compass.** Include alignment to personal values, and empower yourself with symbols of your Ultimate Future.

- **People who can help you.** Identify external support, if applicable. Perhaps you need a mentor or someone who can serve as a connection or a helpful resource for you.

- **Include personal development.** Address any gaps discovered within authenticity and skills needed. Include any behaviors you'd like to see change.

- **Financial, time, and logistical considerations.** Think about constraints and considerations in your plan for finances, timing, and other logistics. If you plan to leave your career to pursue self-employment, have you considered how much financial backing you need? When starting a business, it may take as long as three years to return to a full income. If you're considering returning to school or additional training, what are the application and program timelines?

- **Defining and recognizing success.** Ensure that your plan has a strong vision for success. What is that goal, and how will you recognize that it has been achieved?

Your Action Plan | Exercise 10

The next exercise is an example of a high-level action plan for bringing your Passion forward. Choose the best approach based on your situation. You may already have a personal action plan process that you'd like to leverage. You may want a concrete action plan, or you may prefer a less-structured approach. If less structured is what you're going for, you can read this chapter and skip past Exercise 10 to the Conclusion.

Preparation

- Think about what type of plan you're building. Is this plan to bring your Passion forward, make a career change, or better manage your energy toward what's important to you?

- There are no right answers.

- Start thinking of your goal for the plan and overall timelines. You may elect to build a thirty- or ninety-day plan.

Instructions

(1) Build your action plan. Set a specific, measurable goal for this timeframe. Include a number, a level of quality, or some other measurement so that this goal has a clear and strong meaning for you. What do you want to have by the end of thirty or ninety days?

(2) Outline the necessary areas of focus for the plan in the first column.

(3) Identify specific activities in the second column. Choose your timing, and think about the significance of that item.

(4) Use the Action Plan checklist on the next page to ensure you've covered major areas and considerations.

(5) Once the plan is complete, keep this paper handy or move it to your trusted system, calendar, or task management software.

(6) Cross check with your previous answers for clues:

- **Page 73.** Review Exercise 7, Talent and Skills Builder.

- **Page 81, 85-90.** Review Exercise 8-1 and 8-2, Authenticity.

- **Page 104.** Inputs to your action plan on the previous page. Include essential areas in your plan.

Your Action Plan | Exercise 10 | Checklist

Consider revising the action plan until you are satisfied with your responses below.

Action plan checklist questions

- Does the action plan feel good? If not, what will make it better?

- Does the action plan contain positive language, such as "I will" and "I can" rather than "Don't" or "Stop"?

- Does the action plan include others who can help you in your goal?

- Have you planned for ways to bring your personal values forward across your work areas and at home?

- Have you included stepping stones?

- Have you included planning or brainstorming activities?

- For steps that require a financial component, have you planned how you're going to pay for those steps?

- When you reach the milestone at the end of the action plan, will it be clear you've met your goal?

- Are you celebrating success?

Your Action Plan | Exercise 10 | Example

Table 10. My Action Plan (30-day example)

ACTION PLAN			
30-DAY GOAL	In 30 days, I will bring my Passion forward by establishing consistent healthy habits (completed 20 days out of 30), by feeding my soul with strong relationships around me, and I will share my light with others serving a broader audience in coaching.		
AREA OF FOCUS	**NEXT STEPS**	**TIMING**	**SIGNIFICANCE**
BODY & HEALTH	Go to bed by 10:30PM Tell my immediate family of my health goals for additional support and accountability Hold daily practices for meditation, journaling, and jogging (or yoga on non-jogging days)	Weekdays Once Daily	Putting work before health
RELATIONSHIPS	Deepen a.m./p.m. quality time with family Grow relationships that support me Listen to my intuition and strengthen this skill	Daily Ongoing Daily	Show up. Protect myself from negative influences.
COACHING	Be open and honest; vulnerable Share my story and practice my narrative Respect other's learning at their own pace	Daily Weekly Daily	Watch for perfectionist tendencies, old beliefs and judgment
STEPPING STONES	Catch myself saying "but," and reframe into the positive. Use circles in planning, brainstorming, projects	Daily Daily	Look for opportunity, Leverage what works
INNER COMPASS	Review my inner compass and reflect in my journal on how I'm living in alignment	Weekly	Watch for busyness as an excuse
CELEBRATE	Schedule a long weekend filled with hiking, picnics, taking lots of pictures, and marking off local attractions that the family has wanted to do.	Day 30	Focus more on fun

Your Action Plan | Exercise 10

Table 11. Your Action Plan (30-day template)

YOUR ACTION PLAN			
30-DAY GOAL	In 30 days, I will…		
AREA OF FOCUS	**NEXT STEPS**	**TIMING**	**SIGNIFICANCE**

Required Self-Discovery

Accountability. How are you going to catch yourself when you have setbacks?

Notes

Notes

Chapter 11

BONUS—OVERCOMMITMENT

Real freedom is the ability to pause between stimulus and response and in that pause...choose.
- Rollo May, American existential psychologist

In this chapter, you'll learn:

- How to use a three-step strategy for reducing overcommitment
- Where to find support within your action plan
- How to manage incoming requests with improved decisionmaking

You are entering the Maintenance stage.

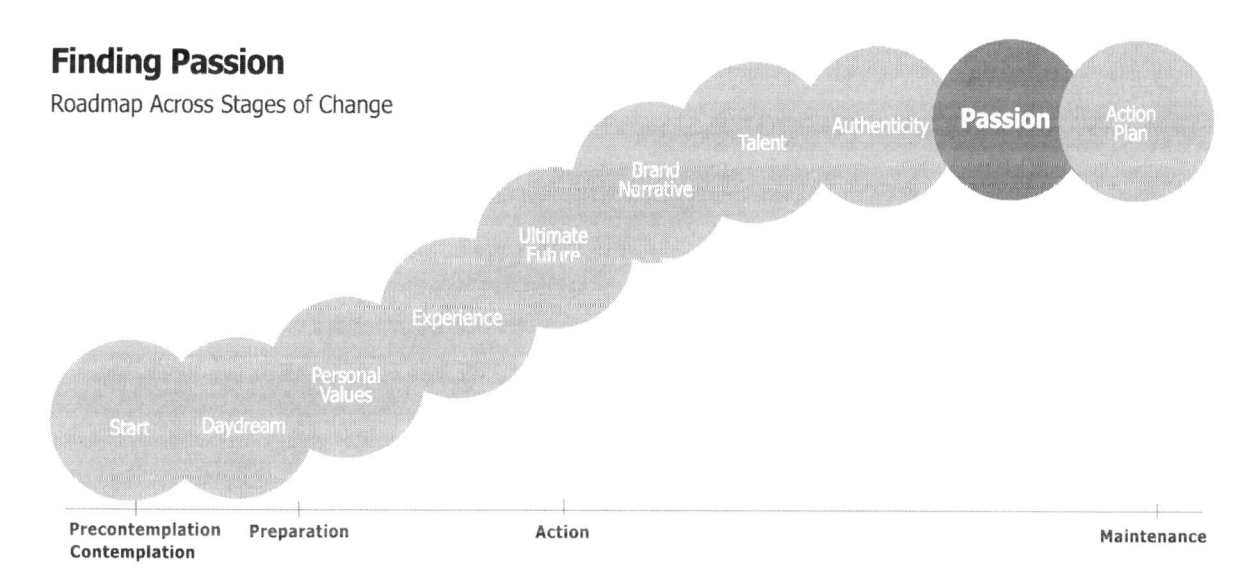

Figure 17. *Finding Passion* Roadmap, beginning steps towards Maintenance.

Overcommitment

Overcommitment is the number one distraction you will face that takes you off plan. To make your action plan stick, you need to expend additional effort to prioritize obligations, new requests and the places where you choose to spend your valuable energy. This chapter helps you clear unnecessary obligations from your work list.

In Resetting Roles Exercise 11, you'll evaluate how additional roles, especially ones that you may not have addressed in the workbook, can be aligned with or out of sync with your goals. This exercise helps you make better decisions, rather than run on autopilot and slip back into old patterns for how you spend your energy.

Resetting Roles | Exercise 11

You've come so far on the journey of finding your Passion that the rest of your major relationships need to get up to speed. Use the following strategy in Resetting Roles to keep you on track to meet your action plan goals.

Preparation

- Use the areas of focus defined in Exercise 10, Your Action Plan, as your guideline to the types of activities that align with your action plan goal.

- You may want to grab a marker and sticky notes if you need more room than a sheet a paper to list the significant and active roles in your life in Step 1 below.

- Significant roles are ones that take more than two hours of your time each month. You can be an employee, a mother or father, a board member, a volunteer, and more.

Instructions

(1) List the significant roles in your life in the column marked "Step 1." If you need additional space, use the subsequent notes pages following the exercise.

(2) List your action plan areas of focus under "Step 2."

(3) Return to the list of roles. In the column marked "Step 3," identify which ones fit into a current area of focus and which ones don't. If the role isn't a match and is one you've been considering stepping out of, write "N/A." You might consider reprioritizing your involvement in this role. Use the notes pages to plan out next steps.

Note: (Ongoing) Mentally check-in with this worksheet anytime you're asked to do something new. If a request doesn't fall into an important role in your life or career plan, suggest to the person an alternative rather than assuming a previous role that takes you away from your Passion.

Resetting Roles | Exercise 11

Table 12. Resetting Roles and mapping to areas of focus

RESETTING ROLES	
STEP 1 ACTIVE ROLES	STEP 3 MAPPING
STEP 2 CURRENT AREAS OF FOCUS	
(1)	
(2)	
(3)	
(4)	
(5)	
(6)	

Required Self-Discovery

Choose. What will you do differently the next time you're asked to do something that's not an area of focus for you?

For roles that no longer align with priorities, outline your next steps below.

Notes

CONCLUSION

Nothing happens without personal transformation.
- W. Edwards Deming

What a journey. When you think back to the date you started this work on page 14, you will see how far you've come from your starting point. Celebrate the fact that your answers came from within you!

You have a choice what to do next. You have new information, new tools by your side, new strengths and increased confidence giving you clarity about your future. Whether you stay in your current position or you share your Passion elsewhere, you can live the life you want now.

What Happened Next?

It's been a whole new existence since I found my Passion. I'm excited about the new balance I've found with staying true to myself and having a career I love. I'm building a business that represents me to the fullest. I'm taking care of myself as never before and by doing so, I'm taking better care of my family. I'm not missing out on these years. I'm no longer numb, but mindful, happy, and full of light. I'm celebrating my amazing life!

While I do sometimes feel stressed, it's not a constant like before. I've got numerous strategies to center myself and not get caught up in urgency or wanting to please others at the expense of my needs. Unlike before, I listen to my intuition when feelings stir.

I haven't thought much about what life would be like had I stayed in my previous career. I suppose too many of the elements of my Passion were missing. There were many nonnegotiables that I knew deep down would never be met. I used to feel restless as if I was on a treadmill to nowhere. That's not for me, not anymore.

Finding my voice, boosting my self-confidence, and loving myself for who I am have made the experience worth it. So I'm not a Senior Manager. That's OK. I'm so much more. I'm real, and there's not a title or label for what that means to me.

> Since writing this book, I've managed to stay balanced working a thirty-five-hour workweek, I unplugged 100% for twelve days on vacation, and I started running to improve my fitness level. There was nothing stopping me from doing this before, only my thinking that got in the way. What keeps me going is making small steps every day, feeling good, and seeing the ripple effect taking care of myself has on my relationships.
>
> One result from this work is that my life-long dream of becoming an author has now come true! A part of my Ultimate Future was within my reach all along, and I'm very proud that I overcame make-believe excuses that held me back.
>
> This is only the beginning of even bigger things to come.

Insights from my self-discovery

I'd like to share with you my best-learned insights:

- **Listen to your intuition no matter what.** When nervous feelings stir, what's your intuition telling you?

- **Continuously improve, at your own pace in life.** Keep learning. Fall down and pick yourself up.

- **Experiment with being out of your comfort zones.** Challenge old thinking and make space for what you want your life to be like.

- **Stay focused on what you want.** Let go of comparing yourself to others.

- **Take on a daily act of courage.** Keep up the momentum toward your Ultimate Future and Passion.

- **Passion.** Your Passion is the answer to what you really want in your life.

Thank you

My wish for you is to keep your commitment to living your Passion every day. In many ways, this commitment is the difference between being happy and always looking back on your life to what could have been. I hope you learn to love the journey, find Passion around every corner, and you live the richest life possible.

Sending you unlimited energy and happiness, I want to thank you for the opportunity to connect with you during this new chapter in your life.

Thank you!

Notes

Appendix

MAINTENANCE PROGRAM

We shall not cease from exploration
And the end of all our exploring
Will be to arrive where we started
And know the place for the first time.
- T.S. Eliot–"Little Gidding"

Maintenance is the stage of change that keeps you moving forward rather than slip back into old patterns and behaviors when managing stressful situations or when making difficult choices. As you gain momentum with your action plan, adding gatekeepers to work with you toward your goal will help you make lasting change.

Maintenance Tips

Seek support when you face overcommitment, negative environments, or disruptions to your routine with the following tips and resources.

Seek a sounding board

Experiment with building support from those around you. Develop a sounding board for the personal and professional work that you're undertaking. Although the learning you've gained to date is mostly private and internal, your maintenance program may involve continuing to communicate your learning with others. Speaking your intentions out loud sets up the action itself. Best of all, having a sounding board gives you needed encouragement, positivity, and recognition as you continue to grow.

Continue to challenge yourself

Leverage any of the strategies in the book to keep you motivated. Daily acts of courage and practices for self-discovery may be ideas that you create some discipline around. If during the exercises you found that a particular idea worked really well for you, consider integrating the tool into your life.

Make action planning into iterative learning

Revisit this body of work every six months. With your next action plan, review *Finding Passion* as part of establishing your thirty- or ninety-day goals to keep you on track. Additional *Finding Passion* workbook exercise pages are available for purchase separately on Amazon.com.

What next?

Consider building in weekly, if not daily, self-reflection time as you plan your goals. If you enjoyed this workbook, the next section suggests further options for you to consider.

More Self-Discovery Tools and Inspiration

Do exercises and tools for self-discovery work really well for you? Build up your toolkit.

Access quick strategies the next time you feel "stuck"

The Managing Mindspaces Toolkit empowers you with ideas, practices and exercises to find fulfillment and use your energy towards what's important. Learn inspiring ways to manage across areas such as motivation, setting boundaries, more about making personal change last and more. You'll love my eInspiration newsletter for the newest tools and tips to live the life you want now.

Sign up or browse at managingmindspaces.com/toolkit.

Daily Act of Courage—Share Your Story

Are you feeling courageous and ready to shout from the rooftops your newfound Passion?

Declare your Passion with others

For many individuals, it is hearing the success stories of others who have faced similar challenges that motivates them to make a life change they've been considering. I invite you to share your story of finding your Passion with others. Your act of courage may make the difference for someone and give you a support network like you've never had before. If you want your vision to happen, you need to declare it. Here's some ideas:

- **Personal brand statement.** Post your statement, and be sure to include the underlying Passion you have in what you do.

- **Personal Values.** Reveal your personal values and express why these words are important to you.

- **Finding Passion.** Share your story, and celebrate the success you've had since reading this book.

Share your story on www.facebook.com/managing-mindspaces or use #FindingPassionBook on Twitter and follow me on @mgingmindspaces.

How to Find a Certified Coach Near You

Would you like to work with a coach for your needs? Here's how to find a top-quality coach in your area.

International Coach Federation certified coaches

The ICF contains resources for those looking for a coach including a directory of members by location, common frequently asked questions, hiring tips and client success stories. The ICF site also contains information on coaching to organizations as well as personal coaching benefits.

To search for credentialed coaches, visit the coach directory at www.coachfederation.org.

Recommended coach matching service

Noomii helps you find the best possible coach for your specific needs. Noomii.com is the "Web's Largest Directory of Life Coaches and Business Coaches." Using their free tool, you can browse coaches located in your area or use their coach matching service to find the best overall coach for your needs. Coaches work in-person or via phone across the globe. Aligned to the standards of coaching defined by the ICF, Noomii coaches are profiled by name, location, speciality, and are verified for their ICF credentials. Look for the ACC, PCC, MCC logos.

To find a specific coach for your needs, visit www.noomii.com.

Managing Mindspaces Personal Coaching Programs

Experience personal coaching working with me as your thinking partner.

Want more self-discovery working directly with me?

Deep dive into the parts of the workbook you found most challenging with someone who understands and has been through this transformation. My program will empower you to find the best solution with you. Working with me, you'll be able to:

- Live with clarity and be yourself more than ever before
- Find fulfillment; Use your energy for what's important, not what's urgent
- Overcome your inner monsters and critic
- Live in alignment to your values on a daily basis

- Make informed decisions, exploring options for today and your long-term career goals

Design your four- or six-month program to get the results you want. Start your personal coaching sessions via phone (or Skype) working directly with me. I'm a member of the ICF, an Associate Certified Coach (ACC), and a Certified Executive Coach (CEC).

You're exactly what I'm looking for in a client who is ready for making a real change in your life. You've come this far using *Finding Passion* on your own. Imagine what's possible if we partnered together?

To secure your spot, visit www.managingmindspaces.com/FindingPassionBook/offer.

Notes

ABOUT THE AUTHOR

Jessica Manca, ACC, CEC, PMP,
is a certified executive coach, entrepreneur,
project management professional and former management consultant.

Jessica left the corporate world and founded Managing Mindspaces in 2012
upon answering the call from her Ultimate Future. She shares her inner light, energy, and inspiration
with others struggling with the dance of well-paying careers that leave them unfulfilled.
She holds an Associate Certified Coach (ACC) credential,
as recognized by the International Coach Federation and received her
Certified Executive Coach (CEC) designation from Royal Roads University.

She practices one-on-one coaching with individuals
across North America, helping others live the lives they want now.

Together with her husband and son, she lives in Vancouver, British Columbia.